I am forever grateful for Hayley Gorcey, whose love, patience and understanding blessed and changed my life.

I also need to thank Rick Rubin for being such an incredible mentor, catalyst and guiding force in my life and Neil Strauss for being an amazing teacher, editor, and friend, and for giving me the courage to write this book.

Finally, a big thank you to Jeremy Brown, Zach Obront, Tucker Max and the whole gang at Book in a Box for helping to make this dream a reality.

KHALIL RAFATI

I FORGOT TO DIE

I FORGOT TO DIE

CHAPTER ONE

Summer 2001

"YOU'RE GOING TO DIE IF YOU DON'T GET HELP."

I'm fading in and out of consciousness, trying to focus my eyes on the figure standing above me.

"If you don't get help, you're going to die!"

Oh shit, I remember this voice. I thought I had simply OD'd again and some overzealous paramedic was trying to hit me with some tough love. No such luck. The voice belongs to my girlfriend's father.

Godammit, why did she let him in?

The voice continues to rant about how irresponsible we are. How could we let this happen again?

Over and over. He's stuck on repeat.

Now my eyes are open but I tune the voice out. I need to assess the situation.

Jennifer's father is here, which means the whole family knows. I slowly make my way toward the bathroom.

Fuck, it looks like a bomb went off in here. Needles and

blood everywhere. I fall into the wall twice. No one seems to notice or care. I rub my shoulder and notice a patch.

Shit, no wonder I'm not sick yet. 150mg Duragesic 72-Hour Timed Release.

Thank God. This will tide me over until Jennifer can get rid of her father and little sister.

I stumble through a cloud of flies toward the toilet. Gatorade bottles are brimming with dark yellow urine. I lift the toilet lid.

Ah, that explains the flies. The landlord must have turned the water off again.

I piss in the sink. The edge is crowded with cuticle clippers, scissors, needle-nose pliers, two bottles of hydrogen peroxide, and one can of paint thinner.

Slowly and carefully I raise my head toward the mirror.

Chunks of flesh are missing from my left cheek and between my eyebrows.

The top part of my right nostril and two patches of my scalp are gone.

On the wall, written in my blood with my hand, are the words:

GOD HELP ME

* * *

I was born in Toledo, Ohio in 1969, the Year of the Cock—the rooster, the bringer of light. I was born premature because, as my mother put it, my father "got excited," which was code for he beat her. My dad was a Palestinian, but the kids at school all called him a "sand nigger," and my mom was a

Polack—both of them straight off the boat.

There was a sad old Indian man who always sat on the street corner. Everybody in my neighborhood was white and they had pretty eyes—blue and green. Everybody was white except my dad and that old Indian man. My dad was brown, but it was an angry brown. The old Indian man was *very* brown, but it was a sad brown that almost seemed more like a red. I was always happy when the rain came because he was so dirty and it made him clean. Everybody else ran but he just sat. *Next time it rains, I'm not gonna run. I'm gonna sit still like the old Indian man and get clean.*

I don't know much about my father's past other than he was born in Jerusalem to a poor Muslim family. I overheard him tell a story once about skipping school as a kid and playing at his cousin's house. When his father found him, he beat the cousin's entire family then made my father run the 12 miles back home while my grandfather rode a bicycle behind him. Every time my dad fell down, my grandfather would get off the bike and beat him.

A relative of mine told me another story in broken English about my dad leaving his first wife and their kids behind in Palestine. He went to Germany to make money and they didn't think he was coming back. When he returned five years later, he found that his brother had married his wife and they'd had a child together.

If my father ever had love in him, by the time I was born it was gone. Life had hardened him. The world, as he knew it, was a bad place.

My mother had it even worse. She was a small child in Poland when World War II broke out. Her father died at sea, fighting the Nazis. Her mother tried to escape to Hungary, but it was very difficult to get through the border and having a child made it nearly impossible, so she left my mom on a stranger's doorstep and the two sisters who lived there took her in. My mother and the sisters were shipped off to Ukraine, Kazakhstan, Uzbekistan, and eventually to Siberia to a labor camp for women and children. My mother never spoke of these times, and when I asked her about it she would always say, "The past is the past and best left alone." But sometimes (rarely) she would mention some details, like being forced to wear a sack around her neck and pick wheat with her bare hands or how 15 or 20 of them lived in one tiny shack with a stove for heat and one bucket that they all had to use to go to the bathroom. Sometimes the bucket would freeze from the cold. Most of them starved to death.

When she was in her thirties, long after the war had ended, my mother and her husband made their way to the United States. They had a son, but soon after, her husband abandoned them and returned to Poland. She managed to track down her biological mother—my grandmother—who was working for a wealthy family as a maid in Toledo, Ohio.

My mom called her.

"I'm coming to see you," she said.

A few days before my mom got to Toledo, her mother closed the garage door and kept the car running. There was never any tearful reunion, answers, or closure. My mom had been abandoned once again. She ended up a single mother working as a maid for the same wealthy family as my grandmother and taking classes at the University of Toledo, where she met my father. They fell in love and quickly married—an angry, violent, yet charming man and a broken, beautiful woman who thought she could change him.

Even the honeymoon didn't last long. The first thing my father did after they got married was make my mother give up her son from her previous relationship because he didn't want to raise another man's child. He made her send him to an orphanage. On countless occasions, she begged my father to let her son come home, but he refused, and eventually she got pregnant with me.

My earliest memories, from before I could even talk, are of recurring nightmares I had. One was of a small, shadowy, demonic figure that chased me relentlessly, wanting to kill me. I inherently knew it was evil, before I had heard anything about good and bad, God and the devil, heaven and hell. The other nightmare was of a giant white ghost that would drag me into my parents' closet, pin me to the floor, and tickle me until I couldn't breathe. I would feel an immense pressure on top of me and I couldn't get up. I'd like to say my memories got better after that, happier, but I'd be lying.

When I was five years old, my mother started pleading incessantly again to bring her other son home. Finally my father relented. I don't know what happened to my brother while he was at that orphanage, but I am certain it was horrible. The first time he touched me was very confusing because I was so desperate for attention, but I knew immediately that something was wrong. Over time, the incidents became more and more aggressive. He was eight years older than I was, a young man going though puberty and confused about his sexuality, and I was just something to experiment on.

When it became constant and I couldn't take it anymore, I ran to my mother for help. She was putting makeup on in the mirror, getting ready to go to my father's restaurant, where they both worked day and night. I cried and tugged at her hand, begging her to make him stop. She brushed me away.

"He's just tickling you," she said.

And that was the end of the conversation.

Soon he began inviting other kids from the neighborhood and let them take turns with me. One of the boys saw what my brother was doing and pulled him off of me. He threw my brother across the room, pinned him down, and began whaling on him.

"What the fuck is wrong with you?!"

He hit him a couple more times and then yelled again, "What the fuck is wrong with you? Why would you do that?!"

Then he realized I was still standing there watching. He looked up at me with these wild blue eyes and said, "It's okay now. Go on, get out of here."

I stood there frozen in awe. I was so happy.

"It's okay now. Go on, get out of here," he repeated, but this time louder.

And I took off running.

His name was Greg Huffman. He lived five houses down the street from us on Laurentide, adjacent to the creek. His mom was this real classy lady who always had on fancy gardening outfits and gloves. She was always gardening. They had the most immaculate landscaping—the greenest grass, the reddest roses—and she was always so pleasant and said hello to everyone. I loved it when Greg came around, which was quite often. He and my brother were pretty close.

Two months went by without my brother touching me again. Then one afternoon, my brother came home, running and panting, out of breath, sobbing, which is something I didn't see him do very often. Greg had been rushed to the hospital for emergency open heart surgery. He passed away that afternoon. How could this happen? Greg was my hero, my protector, not to mention he was only 14 years old. How could God let this happen? How could He take Greg and leave me alone with my brother again? I hated God. I hated the world and everyone in it.

I never told my father about what my brother did to me. We all lived in constant fear of upsetting him. The slightest misstep would send him into a rage, beating all of us and breaking all the furniture. So I didn't dare tell him because I knew I'd just end up getting the shit knocked out of me. The only way to survive in my house was to be invisible.

But I didn't want to be invisible. I wanted to be seen, heard, loved, taught, and appreciated. I wanted what my friends had with their parents and siblings. I could see how different my family was from everyone else's. I saw the other kids out playing catch with their dads, packing the car up to go camping or fishing. I was fucked. I was cursed. Something was wrong with me. *Why had I been born?*

* * *

Even the weather in Toledo was oppressive. The spring and fall were beautiful, but the winters were cold and Godless and unrelenting and the heat and humidity of summer left you in a half-drunken stupor.

Whenever the TV was on in our house, which it almost always was, it was covered with images of death and destruction—the Vietnam War, the Son of Sam, the Hillside Strangler, Jim Jones suicide cult, etc.

Then there was religion. I couldn't have been more confused about the topic. My mother's best friend Basha was also from Poland. We would go to her house on Fridays for Shabbat dinner. During the holidays, we would light the menorah and celebrate Chanukah. It was well understood that anything we did at Basha's house was never to be discussed at home. I kept my mouth shut, but one time my dad showed up there and dragged my mother out by her hair. That was the end of our Jewish traditions.

My father was a Muslim and from time to time he would have other Muslims over as guests. They would go nuts with washing their hands and their faces, then kneel down on these special rugs on the floor and say all kinds of stuff in Arabic over and over again.

"Allah Akbar! Allah Akbar!"

When it came to schooling, there was no way my father was gonna have any son of his go to a public school—that was for poor people and he was a very proud man. The only problem was that all of the private schools were Catholic. And not just Catholic, but Jesuit Catholic.

Catholicism only brought about more alienation and shame. I didn't understand it. All of these creepy priests and angry nuns with their funny outfits. So much pageantry, so much pomp and circumstance, that stinky frankincense, eating the body and drinking the blood of Jesus Christ—it just didn't seem right. I actually really loved the idea of Jesus and very much enjoyed hearing about his teachings. Sometimes I would even pray to him. But the exposure to all these new rituals left me more confused than ever. One thing is for sure—it solidified my belief that I was different and I didn't belong. Sitting, then standing, then kneeling and making the sign of the cross had my head spinning with doubt and self-hatred.

The pressure was building and something was bound to break.

It happened a few months into first grade at St. Pat's. My teacher was a former nun, very strict and composed, and she was giving us a talking-to about the new Christmas tree at the front of the room. It was a beautiful tree, decorated with glass bulbs and handmade ornaments.

"No one is to touch or go near the tree," she said, scanning the room to make sure everyone understood. "Each one of these ornaments…"

Her voice faded out as I stood up and began walking towards the tree. I could feel every eye in the room on me, and it felt like I was even watching myself as I stopped right in front of the tree and, with one quick shove, knocked the entire thing over. The sound was enormous, much louder than I'd expected. Bulbs exploded and glass ornaments shattered. Wooden pieces skidded across the floor.

The teacher gasped, then stood frozen in shock and horror.

I still felt separated from myself, watching it happen with all the other kids, our jaws dropping in astonishment. But I also felt relieved, like the lid had been taken off the pressure cooker.

The teacher lunged at me. She grabbed my arm and started yelling as she spanked me. I began to laugh. I tried to keep it inside but couldn't. It started quietly but quickly grew into loud and uncontrollable laughter. Some of the other kids, mostly boys, began laughing as well. This threw our teacher into a frenzy. She spanked harder and harder but this only made me laugh more. She eventually exhausted herself. Her hand hurt more than I did. Out of breath, broken and defeated, she ordered me to the principal's office.

I should have felt bad. Ashamed. But I was exhilarated. I'd found my first drug, my first addiction: defiance.

*　*　*

I used to beg my mother on my knees to divorce my father. When I was seven, my dream came true. My mother had finally had enough. She and I stayed in the house and my father moved out. My brother went off to school at the United States Naval Academy, which should have made me feel better, but I simply became numb. Numb to all of it, to everything. There was a busy street that ran perpendicular to my house that I would ride my bike across, pedaling as fast as I could without looking in either direction to check for oncoming traffic. Cars would slam on their brakes and beep their horns, which put a smile on my face so big that it hurt. I guess I was more excited about the idea of risking my life intentionally than dying slowly, painfully, suffocating from lack of love and self-worth. It wasn't really a death wish, more of a "fuck you" to God for putting me in this position— in this life, in this family, in this town.

My mother dropped out of nursing school and got a job at the local hospital during the graveyard shift. I never really saw her. She took sleeping pills during the day and was gone all night. When I woke up, there was always $5 on the table.

Most days I took that $5 and went to the snack bar at the country club. I loved spending time there, eating and play-ing in the creek. I *loved* being in the sun. I would show up the first day it opened in the spring and go every day until it closed in the fall.

The janitor at the club was a guy named Tommy. He was

22 years old, had long brown hair, and was the coolest guy I had ever met. He rarely talked to anybody—he just kept to himself and did his work. One day I was walking behind him on my way out and I saw a giant Coca-Cola truck parked out front. Tommy slowly and casually walked toward the truck. He stopped abruptly and turned around to see if anyone was looking and saw me standing there. He cracked this great big Cheshire cat grin and pulled a knife out from his jean shorts. It was a butterfly knife. He opened it methodically and with great skill, locking the safety with his thumb, and then swiftly drove it into one of the massive black tires. The tire let out a loud gasping sound, but no one was around to notice except for me. He was my hero.

After that, I made a habit of hopping the fence at night, after the club closed, and Tommy and I would smoke cigarettes. We lay on the lounge chairs on those hot, balmy evenings, staring up at the stars and listening to the incessant sounds of the cicadas, putting us in a trance-like state. I told Tommy about some of my troubles, but never in great detail. And he would just listen.

That was the safest I'd ever felt. I never wanted those nights to end. I always fell asleep and sometimes Tommy would, too, until eventually he'd wake me up: "C'mon, kid, you gotta get home."

The club was my sanctuary. I even joined the swim team there when I was eight years old. When I was 10 a new coach named Brian was hired. Brian was a charismatic and charming man in his mid-thirties who had a beautiful girlfriend and his job was to spend time out in the sun at the pool all day. I really looked up to him. I wanted to *be* him.

The following year, Brian said he wanted to take me

camping, something I had never done before. I couldn't wait to go, but I was also a little bit torn about it. Several times after swim practice, when all of the other kids had gone home, I didn't have anywhere to go, so I would sit in the Jacuzzi to stay warm. He would come keep me company, but had this bizarre habit of putting his hand between my legs and asking me if I wanted to play a game of "Sharkie." I would always back away and laugh it off. My instinct was to punch him in the face, but I really looked up to him and, to be honest, really enjoyed the company, so I brushed it off.

I agreed to go camping, somewhat reluctantly. My excitement over doing something that I had never done before—and, I suppose, a pretty good deal of denial—superseded my gut instinct. Turns out Brian had a very specific reason for wanting to take me camping: he wanted to get me alone, out into the woods, far enough away that no one could hear me scream for help.

The man I'd looked up to and trusted not only tore that away from me, he took away the one place I could go to feel safe and be a kid. I stopped going to swim practice and competitions.

I wanted to tell Tommy, but...

At the end of that August, I was awoken by a loud pounding on my front door. I thought it must be my friend Teddy, but it wasn't. It was my friend Megan. She had just gotten her license and had driven over to pick me up. I opened the door and Megan, giggling loudly, said, "Did you hear what happened to that janitor guy?"

"Tommy?" I asked.

"Yeah," she said, "I guess so. The janitor."

"What? What are you talking about?"

"He died."

"What the fuck are you talking about?"

"He died," she said, laughing nervously.

"What the fuck are you talking about, you stupid bitch?! He didn't die! I saw him last night."

"He died. Gosh, what's your problem?"

"He didn't fucking die!" My throat was constricting, my eyes burning.

"He did too, you douche bag! He fell off a ladder and broke his neck."

I slammed the door in Megan's face. I heard her car speed off as I fought back the tears. I went in my room and shut the door. I was scared I would explode. I crouched down behind my bed, kneeling on the floor.

"No, no, no..." I clenched my teeth and growled. "No, no, no..."

I started to punch myself in my legs—first my thighs, then my calves. "No! No! No!"

Any remaining fragments of childhood innocence that were left in me disintegrated. I had been left to rot in this dark, incomprehensible reality. Everyone I met was either going to die or do something terrible to me. After that, I turned bad. My insides turned bad. My soul turned black.

✳ ✳ ✳

I started getting into all sorts of trouble at school—fights, vandalism, skipping class, bad grades. They failed me for the first time in sixth grade and having to repeat it was like pouring kerosene on my bonfire of shame and alienation. I couldn't take much more of this life.

In the Ohio of the '70s and '80s, it wasn't unheard of for kids to go to the liquor store and buy cigarettes or booze for their parents. One day I went with my best friend Teddy Papenhagen to buy cigarettes for his mom. We added three bottles of Mad Dog 20/20 to the purchase, then took them into the woods and got blind drunk. We stumbled our way back to an Arby's and devoured a massive amount of French fries—which Teddy hoped would absorb some of the alcohol so his mom didn't see how smashed he was. I didn't share those concerns. I *loved* being drunk. It was the greatest. I felt strong and safe and powerful. Invincible, really. Booze was my new best friend.

After that I got drunk almost every weekend. The kids in the neighborhood had figured out my mom left at 10:30 every night and that the house had no adult supervision. And I'm not talking about the good kids. These were kids like me, neglected and ignored, looking for any way to feel like they belonged. If someone offered me a cup, a can, or a bottle, I drank it. Then they started offering me pills—Yellow Jackets, Black Beauties, whatever—and I'd swallow them.

I was 12 years old the first time I had intercourse with a girl. It felt really great when it was happening, but I remember going home, getting in the shower, and sobbing. I felt dirty, like I had crossed some sort of invisible line that I shouldn't have—not at that age, anyway. After that, if a girl wanted to have sex with me, I would. She didn't have to be pretty or skinny—any girl would do.

I always had a girlfriend and I always cheated on them. My new addiction, feeling wanted, became the most intense drug of all.

* * *

The weekends were a blur of partying. Sometimes it spilled over into the next week. I was in my second year of sixth grade and I can remember many times when I would show up Monday morning still drunk from the night before.

Early one morning, after I had stayed up all night on Dexedrine, I lay in bed for hours trying to fall asleep. I had missed school the day before and I never liked to miss school two days in a row because then it would draw attention and questions were asked. My heart was racing so bad it felt like it was gonna jump out of my chest. I had done too much, something that would eventually become a theme in my life. I heard the garage door open, which meant my mother was home from work and it was time to jump up and get ready for school.

I got out of bed and took a shower to get rid of the cigarette smell. I quickly got dressed and avoided my mother as I carefully slipped out the door. On my way out, I grabbed a two-liter bottle of Pepsi out of the refrigerator and some gummy bears out of the drawer. I often drank Pepsi for breakfast—this was during the Pepsi and Coke war, and Coke hadn't won yet. I took the two-liter to the bus stop with me. It was freezing cold outside, but my body and breath were hot from the amphetamines, sugar, and caffeine that were coursing through my veins. I felt off, to say the least.

The bus ride was a blur. When I got to school, I had the stark realization that it was Tuesday. Tuesdays we went to Mass first thing in the morning. I felt sick and incredibly nervous. My body was hot and cold at the same time. At Mass, I took my seat in the pew and a wave of panic washed over me, unlike any I had felt before. It was quiet, too quiet. My heart started thumping in my chest loudly. I could feel it. I could hear it. It felt like I was falling backwards. My impulse was to scream, but I knew that would be disastrous. I pictured them dragging me off—the nuns, the priests, the overweight lunch mothers. I pictured them putting me in a straightjacket and locking me in a rubber room. There was a flash like lightning and then again the feeling that I was falling backwards quickly. I couldn't breathe. My friend Joe Ostephy was sitting next to me. He was a funny kid with unusual features—big lips, big ears—but girls loved him. I grabbed his leg and I whispered, "Shit man, I'm losing it."

"What?" he asked.

"Shhh...." The teacher shot us a glare.

I leaned back into my pew, fists and teeth clenched, my abdomen constricted. Again I whispered, "I think I'm losing it." I stood halfway up, preparing to make a run for it. Joe put his hand up and with a grin on his face said, "Sit down. *Sit down*. What are you doing?" I sat back down and felt a shooting pain in my ass.

"Ouch!!!"

Joe immediately began to crack up, as did some of the other kids. He had sneaked a thumb tack onto my pew. The pain was intense. The laughter was disrupting. But as the teacher stood up and ordered both of us off to the principal's office, I noticed that the panicked feeling was gone. I no longer heard my heart. I no longer felt like I was falling backwards off of a chair. In that instant I learned that if I could somehow distract myself, I might have a fighting chance at combating whatever storm of mental illness was brewing inside of me.

Being drunk or high seemed to keep the panic attacks under control and I was determined to have people around me, any people, just so I could stay distracted. And everything was great, until they started leaving. Eventually I'd be alone again. I couldn't sleep and would stay up all night watching TV by myself. I had this crazy make-believe fantasy that Johnny Carson was my father. I put a great deal of effort into creating and maintaining this illusion. It started when I was much younger, maybe when I was five years old, and I maintained it into my late teens. Thank God for Johnny Carson.

We only had four channels—ABC, NBC, CBS, and PBS— and once David Letterman signed off, they played the National Anthem and cut to what I called the Ant Races. Just static. Then I was alone again.

When I was alone, when I was vulnerable, the attacks were unbearable. They came on like a freight train. I couldn't even leave the house. I'd lay on the sofa, my body writhing uncontrollably, hyperventilating, fists clenching, teeth grinding, abdomen constricted, laying in the fetal position, rocking back and forth. At some point I discovered that if I bit my hand hard enough, the attacks would sometimes lessen or subside completely, but other times all I could do was grab this hideous, heavy wool blanket we had and cover myself on the sofa until the attack passed. I'd lay there under the blanket, biting my hand and crying out to God for help, and when it didn't come, I'd yell, "Fuck you! Why are you doing this to me?"

During the worst attacks I'd just pray for death.

But something amazing happened in 1982: I got cable TV and Atari. Teddy got Activision. We discovered MTV. The world changed. Knowing these escapes were there for me at any time of the day lifted a huge burden. A few other things that brought levity to my unbearable childhood existence:

watching John McEnroe play tennis, Eddie Murphy's standup comedy routine *Delirious*, punk rock, the movies *Valley Girl* and *Fast Times at Ridgemont High*, Michael Jackson's *Thriller* video, breakdancing, and the love and friendship of a girl named Kori Keefer.

But still there were times when the only way to get through the night was to get blackout drunk. On way too many occasions, my mom came home from work to find vomit everywhere and me passed out with puke all over my face. She would yell and scream about the mess and the fact that I could have choked to death.

But the truth is, if I hadn't had those coping mechanisms and means for connecting with other human beings, I probably would have killed myself. My classmate, Charlie War, had taken his own life when we'd been in fourth grade. He had sat right next to me and we'd been pretty good friends. Losing him was really sad, but it also planted the seed that I ultimately was in control and if I really needed to, I could turn out the lights permanently.

✳   ✳   ✳

When I was 12 years old, I asked my father for a pair of $60 Nike shoes for breakdancing.

"You have shoes," he said. "You don't need another pair of goddam shoes."

"Yes I do," I said. I didn't, but I really wanted them and was going to be a pain in the ass until I got them. This broke out into an argument that ended in one of his famous backhands, which always came with the added pain of the solid gold Presidential Rolex he wore on his left wrist. We didn't speak again for days.

One night soon after that, he took me to my favorite restaurant, the Oak'en Bucket, which was owned by the most charismatic and hilarious man I've ever met, who was named Gus. I don't know what other kids felt like when they went to Disneyland because I never went, but I imagined it to be something like what I felt when I went to the Oak'en Bucket. The place was thick with cigarette smoke and filled with characters right out of a Martin Scorsese film: Tommy "Scarface" Buyers, Leo "the Pimp," Ricky "the Hit Man" Scavianno, Miami Mike, Billy Scott, and Butch Wilson. Gus was half Sicilian and half Greek and his mother had direct ties to the infamous Purple Gang of Detroit. He always denied being involved with the Mafia, but there was no mistaking that these other guys were. They all drove Cadillacs and Oldsmobile Toronados, carried giant bankrolls of cash, and wore tons of gold jewelry. Some of them even wore floor-length fur coats. I was fascinated. I really looked up to these guys. Gus was so confident—he always had everyone laughing. I wanted to be just like him when I grew up.

Gus knew my family well and stopped by the table to say hello. He could tell there was tension between me and my father. I wouldn't even look up.

He asked my father, "What's wrong with him?"

"He wants a $60 pair of goddam shoes."

Gus reached into his pocket and pulled out a wad of cash. That was just the kind of guy he was.

My father slammed his hand on the table. "Don't give him a penny! If you want to help him, give him a job."

Gus laughed and asked me, "You want a job?"

I sat up straight. "Yes."

"Are you serious?" Gus laughed.

"Yes!" I was partially saying it to bluff my father, but I was also intrigued by the idea of hanging around Gus and the Oak'en Bucket more.

"Come here tomorrow afternoon," Gus said. "Be here by 4:30."

I showed up the following day an hour early and they handed me a giant rubber apron which was way too big for a 5'1" 12-year-old and I swear that thing must've weighed 25 pounds. We had to tie a special knot in the back to stop it from dragging on the floor and tripping me. But I had a job and I was happy. I got paid $6 an hour. I made $36 that Friday night and $42 on Saturday. Sunday morning, I proudly walked to Southwyck Mall and marched right into the Foot Locker. I spoke clearly and with authority to the man twice my age who was working there: "Grab me a size 6-1/2 in the bright red Nike High Tops with the Velcro straps."

I felt like a millionaire when I put those shoes on! And I learned something very valuable that day: if you want something, go work for it.

So I worked, partly for the money and partly to escape my house. But it didn't stop me from getting into trouble. I got arrested for the first time at 12 years old for vandalism.

I'd been caught shoplifting at a record store before that, but the owners called my mother instead of the cops. She'd apologized profusely for my behavior, paid for the stolen record, and driven me home in silence, and that had been the end of that. This time was different. A few buddies and I broke into a house while the owners were away on summer vacation. I didn't intend to steal anything—I just wanted that adrenaline rush. We made ourselves comfortable in the living room, drank way too much, and then trashed the place like we were Led Zeppelin at the Chateau Marmont. Afterward, one of the guys got caught with a stolen Walkman by his mom. She called the police and he told them I stole it, which was a complete lie. I was pissed.

They took me down to the police station and put me in an interrogation room. They didn't have any real evidence against me so they let me go, but first they asked me a bunch of questions and scared the shit out of me, which is exactly what they wanted to do.

But it didn't stick

* * *

When I was 14, my father moved back into the house and kicked my mother out. She had to get an apartment and I spent the majority of my time there, driving her crazy with all the trouble I got into. Finally, one of her friends sat me down and told me I wasn't welcome there anymore. I was to leave and never come back.

That left me staying with my father. I didn't last two weeks. I got into a fight with a boy at school named Billy Lucius. I told him to tell his friend to meet me after class because I was gonna kick his ass. Billy punched me right in the face. He was a wrestler and he dove for my legs to try to take me down. I jumped back, grabbed his head, and began smashing it into the metal chalkboard ledge. Everything else was a blur. By the time the four lunch mothers tackled me to the ground, I was covered in blood.

Billy was taken to the hospital and I was, yet again, dragged down to the principal's office. After much debate about whether or not to call the police, they called my father. I was immediately expelled from school, which was fine with me because I hated that fucking school.

What Billy could not do to me, my father certainly made up for. I almost ended up in the hospital, too. I went out that night and came back early in the morning to find the locks had been changed. That's how he let me know I didn't have a home anymore. The only place I had left to go was work, so I went to the Oak'en Bucket and told Gus what was going on.

"Well," he said, "you can go stay with my daughter and ex-wife."

This seemed too good to be true, but for some reason they let me move in. I wasn't about to question why. Nicole was a year younger than I was and we were already really close because we went to school together. Her mother, Debbie, was the coolest mom anyone knew. The fridge was always stocked, Debbie cooked breakfast on the weekends, and she let us stay out as late as we wanted, never asking what we were up to.

Things were looking up. I didn't *need* to get drunk all the time, but when I did I drank to the point of blacking out. There were tons of girls, even more so as we began freshman year. Nicole went to the all-girls Catholic school St. Ursula, which opened all kinds of new possibilities for me. And I went to the all-boys private high school St. John's. But as good as it was living with Debbie and Nicole, I knew it was far from normal and a direct result of no one else wanting me around.

When I was 15, I was arrested for the last time—as a teenager, anyway.

I was with Teddy again—sober, surprisingly—and his

older brother was driving us to McDonald's. He had a broken shotgun in the back seat that he was taking to get fixed. I barely even noticed the gun until we passed three kids on skateboards who yelled something at us and flipped us off.

"Stop the car!" I yelled. The car stopped and I jumped out with the shotgun. "What did you say, motherfuckers?"

I pumped it even though it wasn't loaded. The cocking mechanism made a very loud *click-clock* sound. The kids took off in complete terror. I laughed, got back in the car, and we went to McDonald's. We were on our way back and just about to turn onto Teddy's street when I yelled, "Keep going!"

There were about 15 cop cars lining the street. One of them peeled out when they saw us and the chase was on. My heart was racing as Teddy's brother sped up. We got around a few corners before the cops caught up and I jumped out of the car while it was still moving to hide in some pricker bushes. I didn't have shoes or a shirt on and the bushes cut into every inch of exposed skin. But the cops didn't find me. They searched the neighborhood for hours before finally giving up.

What was I supposed to do then? I couldn't go to Debbie and Nicole's. I didn't want them to know the cops were after me. So I crept back toward my father's house, peeking around every corner and ready to bolt at any second, but I made it without seeing any police cars. Thankfully I didn't see my father, either. I climbed through an open window and went straight to my old room, scared shitless but intoxicated by the thrill of having pulled it off.

About an hour later I heard the phone ring, then the loud and heavy Arabic accent of my father echoing down the hall: "Khalil?"

Shit. "Yeah?"

"Stay there, don't move."

Fuck!

A few minutes later the police pulled into the driveway. My father went out to meet them. He turned around and came charging toward the house like a bull. He took me to the ground with one open-handed slap to the top of my head and then dragged me outside by my hair. "Take him out to the field and beat the shit out of him. Then take him to jail."

I could tell by the look on the officers' faces that they felt bad for me. I spent that night in a jail cell wondering what was going to happen to me. My mom showed up the next day and told me I was being charged with attempted murder. The previous times I had been arrested, the charges were dropped immediately and I got off with probation. This time, no such luck.

"The gun wasn't even loaded!" I yelled. "It doesn't even work!"

I was offered a plea bargain of aggravated menacing, which I plead guilty to. The silver lining was that because I was a minor, they put the charge into a sealed record. As long as I didn't get arrested again before I turned 18, the charge would be erased completely.

I'd missed work, which meant I had to tell Gus about the incident. He tried being serious and giving me a talking to, but he kept cracking up and making me recount the story. He loved the fact that I had gotten away from all of those cops and I could tell that he was bummed that my dad had turned me in. He made sure I could go back and stay with Nicole and Debbie, which was a huge relief. As I turned to walk out of the room with my head bowed in shame, Gus said "Hey, kid—here, take this" and he handed me cash. I can't remember how much, I just remember feeling such relief. No, it wasn't relief—it was exhilaration. I had never had that much cash in my hands before. I stared down at it intently and he patted me on the shoulder and said, "Go on, go home now." I began to cry as I walked out the door, making sure he didn't see me.

*　*　*

I lasted almost all of freshman year at St. John's. I caused lots of problems and was acting out more and more, but I was getting much better at not being caught. This lasted until early spring, at one of the dances being held by another all-girls school called Notre Dame. By this time, I had learned that when two large groups of guys were about to fight, if you could find the biggest, loudest one and throw the first punch, you would scare the shit out of all the other guys and most likely win the fight. This was a priceless skill because I was not a good fighter, just crazy and stupid with nothing to lose. It helped me to solidify a reputation for being tough—that, along with the fact that I began emulating Gus and his cohorts by slicking my hair straight back, infusing my speech with a slight but affected tough guy accent, and carrying around a giant bank roll (mostly fives, tens, and twenties, but always covered by a hundred).

So here I was at this dance and a bunch of guys from our rival high school, St. Francis, gathered together and began taunting us, shooting us dirty looks while they pointed and laughed. There was no shortage of girls and certainly no reason to fight, but that's just what we did. It was Ohio, after all. What else were we gonna do? I saw the biggest and loudest guy and quickly moved toward him.

Unfortunately, one of the nuns who had been watching me saw exactly what I was about to do and went to step in front of me. I had too much momentum going to stop. I put my arm out and pushed her aside and followed through with a right handed punch, which landed square on the jaw of that biggest and loudest guy. There was a brief scuffle followed by some loud gasps. Everyone stood still and when I turned around, the nun was laying flat on her back. My intentions were only to push her out of my way, but she had fallen to the ground...hard.

Someone yelled "Call the police!" and my friends and I quickly ran out.

The following Monday morning I was expelled from St. John's High School. Again, I told Gus and again, he began laughing uncontrollably. He kept stopping me and making me start over from the beginning, laughing louder and louder every time.

"You hit a nun?!"

"No!" I yelled. "I didn't hit a nun!"

He just kept repeating it to himself and laughing. "What the fuck is wrong with you? Why would you hit a nun?!"

I realized after a while that he knew I didn't hit the nun. He just couldn't resist the opportunity to amuse himself.

The following weekend, a friend of mine named Pete Handwork invited me to stay the night at his house.

"Are you sure?" I asked him.

"What do you mean, am I sure? Of course I'm sure."

So we went to a party, got drunk, I smoked my cigarettes, and afterwards we went back to his house. I woke up in their guest room Saturday morning in my dirty, smoky clothes and Pete was gone. There were loud voices coming from down the hall so I wandered that way, hungover and in desperate need of a shower. The noise was coming from his parents' room, and when I walked past, one of Pete's sisters said, "There he is!"

I looked in and couldn't believe what I saw. Pete and his two younger sisters were in this giant, fluffy white bed with their mom and dad watching Saturday morning cartoons. They all had on matching pajamas and the whole scene looked like an L.L. Bean ad. Everyone was so happy and clean. The kids were happy, the mom and dad were happy, the dog was wagging its tail. I was stunned.

Pete's mom smiled at me. "Come on up!"

"No, no," I said. I was dirty and hadn't brushed my teeth and I didn't want them to smell me—I smelled like cigarette smoke and shame. I didn't belong in that beautiful white bed. I just stood there, frozen.

Pete's parents were great. They talked to me as I stood in the room, a safe distance away from the bed, asked me questions, and actually cared about the answers. I was on the verge of tears the entire time. I didn't want to believe something like that existed. Seeing what Pete had—what I imagined *everybody* had—cracked me open and tore my heart in half.

I dwelled on it for months, thinking about them, all happy in that bed, feeling love, feeling the opposite of what I felt. I was cursed. I had fucked-up parents and a fucked-up life and I was never gonna be okay. Life was catching up with me and I had to get the fuck out of there. I knew I was too much of a chicken shit to shoot myself in the head. I thought many times about crashing my car into a wall or driving it off a bridge, but I was terrified that I would fuck that up, too, and end up in a wheelchair or something. Then there was all of that bullshit they'd taught me in Catholic school about eternal damnation, Purgatory, brimstone and fire. So there I was, cursed with a rotten soul and too scared to put an end to it. Maybe there was a God, but he sure as fuck didn't care about me. I had to get out of there. I had to escape.

CHAPTER TWO

I GOT MY FIRST REAL TASTE OF WHAT LIFE COULD BE LIKE outside of Toledo when I was 16. Of course I'd been beyond the city limits before, but this was the first time I got to go with a friend, a coworker of mine named Tony Song. Tony was the Korean version of Eddie Haskell. I happened to be staying with my father that night, during a short-lived return to his house in hopes of reconciling our relationship. He had remarried for the fourth or fifth time (I don't actually know) to this beautiful Korean woman named Tong, who happened to be best friends with Tony Song's mother. Tony showed up and charmed the socks off them. He acted like a good, studious Asian kid with impeccable manners and my father was impressed.

Tony said, "Khalil and I are going to go back to my house and study for the test."

"Okay, Tony. You guys have a good time."

I was completely baffled. First off, my father was letting me leave with a friend on a school night. Unprecedented. But it was Tony, so I kind of understood. What still confused me was the fact that Tony and I didn't have any classes together, I didn't have a test coming up, and even if I did I sure as hell wouldn't study for it. I was a straight D student who only passed each grade because the teachers didn't want to deal with me again.

When we got in his car—a BMW 525i—I said, "What are you talking about? What test?"

Tony said, "Don't worry about it." He laughed and pulled out a flask. "Here."

I drank it without hesitation. I don't know what it was, but it was harsh. Tony started driving and we were so engrossed in talking and drinking that I didn't even notice when we got on the I-75 North. Eventually I gathered my bearings and asked, "Dude, where the fuck are we going?"

"Don't worry about it. Drink."

Forty minutes later we were in Detroit. Tony thought it was hilarious that I had no idea what was going on. We were driving down desolate, seemingly abandoned streets in downtown Detroit with empty buildings looming all around us and snow blowing everywhere. He finally parked and we walked through the snow into an alley between two big, brick buildings. There weren't any signs or lights. All I could see was a bunch of people standing around talking and smoking. They all wore black clothes.

Tony pushed through the crowd to a door. A huge guy was there checking IDs.

I grabbed Tony. "I don't have a fake ID, man."

Tony laughed again. I felt on the verge of a panic attack as we got closer to the massive doorman. As soon as it was our turn, he said, "How old are you guys?"

"Fifty," Tony said, as he slipped the doorman a $50 bill.

"All right," he said, "go right ahead."

I was still in awe when we walked inside and went down into the basement of this dark, ominous building. The cellar was a big, open space with clouds of smoke swirling in the blacklight. It was so fucking cool. The music pounded against my chest. I'd never heard the song before but it mesmerized me. It resonated with every cell in my body.

> *A change of speed, a change of style.*
> *A change of scene, with no regrets,*
> *A chance to watch, admire the distance,*
> *Still occupied, though you forget.*
> *Different colors, different shades,*
> *Over each mistakes were made.*
> *I took the blame.*
> *Directionless so plain to see,*
> *A loaded gun won't set you free.*
> *So you say.*
> *We'll share a drink and step outside,*
> *An angry voice and one who cried,*
> *'We'll give you everything and more,*
> *The strain's too much, can't take much more.'*
> *I've walked on water, run through fire,*
> *Can't seem to feel it anymore.*
> *It was me, waiting for me,*
> *Hoping for something more,*
> *Me, seeing me this time,*
> *Hoping for something else.*

This was *real* music, not the garbage they played on WIOT in Toledo (Journey, REO Speedwagon, Foreigner). I never understood what the fuck those bands were talking about anyway and I didn't care. In that moment, I was reborn, unafraid, and liberated. The words were sung so I didn't have to say them. It was Ian Curtis who had died for my sins, not Jesus Christ. I always figured I'd burn in hell, but at least now I knew I'd have company. In that dark, abandoned basement on that night, and many others like it, my life was saved, but this time in a much more profound way. I discovered music: The Cure, Sisters of Mercy, The Smiths, Front 242, The Cult, Communards, etc. I listened with complete strangers who were closer to me than anyone had ever been. They understood exactly who and what I was, and I knew them. The bands were singing the songs of my heart, my sorrow, my isolation, my story. A tremendous sense of relief flooded through me. It was baptism by fire.

We stayed until the place closed down early the next morning. As Tony and I left, exhausted and glowing, I finally found out what the place was called: The Shelter.

Of course.

❊ ❊ ❊

Over the next few years, I went there as often as I could, even more so after I dropped out of high school. After getting kicked out of St. John's, I'd wound up at a public high school called Bowsher. I'd failed class after class, but because there had been a lot of other troubled kids there as well, I had no longer stuck out like a sore thumb. But it was too late. The truth is that once they'd held me back in sixth grade, I had just given up. There hadn't been a week that had gone by where I hadn't missed at least one day of school, but often it had been more than that. I had become completely dis-enchanted with the entire educational process. Halfway through senior year, I had dropped out of school altogether. It had just become too much of a hassle.

When I wasn't at The Shelter, I often went to see live music—Echo and the Bunnymen in Ann Arbor, Depeche Mode in Detroit. One night I saw New Order, Public Image Limited, and the Sugar Cubes all on one bill at an outdoor venue outside Detroit. It was amazing how good I felt when I was immersed in music compared to how shitty I felt in my day-to-day existence. Music changed everything. It became a coping mechanism and a means of escape, but in reality I was still stuck in Toledo, Ohio.

By my late teens, I'd fully registered most of the stuff that had happened to me when I was younger—the sexual, emo-tional, and physical abuse; the neglect—and resigned myself to the fact that it was going to be with me forever. And even though the music I loved was cathartic and resonant, it was also pretty bleak and it fed my depression. My panic attacks had subsided for the most part only to be replaced by a con-stant, crushing depression and overwhelming self-loathing.

The only thing that made me feel better was to act out, the more intense and dangerous the better. I craved the dis-traction that the adrenaline rush provided. I got into dealing pot, selling stolen merchandise, and arson. I was part of a bad scene that was getting worse, and it never crossed my mind to worry about dying. I was too busy dreading the thought of living this way forever. The future wasn't worth being around for.

Then in 1987, not a moment too soon, I got invited to California. I was 17 and a friend of mine named Kenny who was going to art school on the west coast asked me to come out and spend a few days with him, then drive back to Toledo together. Going from Ohio to California, even for just 72 hours, was like upgrading from black and white to Technicolor. The tiny glimpse of what life could be like there was intoxicating. California is where everything was happening: music, movies, models. I wanted so badly to be a part of it.

A few years passed and I ran my mouth all the time about moving to California. It was like a mantra. It quickly turned into background noise, even to me. I fantasized often about moving there, but I carried on with my same routines, same shitty jobs, same misery, same self-destructive behavior. I was nearly 21 when my girlfriend (one of them, anyway) Claudia and I went to see the movie *The Doors*. When Val Kilmer and his on-screen bandmates sang "This is the End," I was transfixed. They were singing directly to me:

> *The west is the best*
> *The west is the best*
> *Get here and we'll do the rest*

I turned to Claudia and whispered, "I have to go."

"You have to go to the bathroom?"

"No," I said, "I have to go. I have to get out of here. I have to go to California."

She nodded politely. I felt like I was speaking with the conviction of pure truth and revelation, but she'd heard it before. I'd like to say I went home, packed, and left that night. But I didn't. I didn't have the guts.

I started drinking even more to put out the fire inside me, but it was like drinking gasoline. The fire only got bigger and hotter. My entire week revolved around partying. Tuesday nights I'd drag my friends to a club called Upstairs Downstairs in Bowling Green. Thursdays we'd go to Ann Arbor and hit the Nectarine Ballroom. Fridays it was Nikki's Tavern and The Shelter in Detroit. I'd dance like a lunatic, losing myself to the music and inevitably bumping into the wrong person and starting a fight. I didn't care. More fuel for the fire.

When I drank I always tried to find the balance between oblivion and lucidity. I rarely hit the mark. Instead, I'd be on my knees or curled up in the fetal position on the bathroom floor at 3:00 a.m. with the room spinning, worshipping the porcelain God.

A year after *The Doors,* I was at a wedding with a bunch of friends. I drank with a vengeance because I felt like everyone was staring at me like I didn't belong—"Oh, *that* guy's here?"—and my defense was to drink more and get louder. Finally I'd had enough of the dirty looks and stood up.

"Fuck this. Let's go. Let's go to Detroit."

Five friends and I piled into a car and I drove like a lunatic to The Shelter. We drank all the way there and kept drinking once we arrived, which was a miracle. When The Shelter closed, we stumbled to Greektown in search of an open bar, half of us stopping to puke along the way. In my drunken stupor I had a flash of inspiration and jumped onto the hood of a parked car.

"We've gotta get the fuck outta here! We're gonna die in this fucking town! Do you guys want to die in this shitty little fucking town that we live in or do you want to go live life? Let's get the fuck outta here! I'm getting the fuck outta here."

All my friends just laughed. "You're not going anywhere."

"The fuck I'm not," I said. "I'm leaving."

"Yeah? Where you gonna go?"

"I'm going to California," I said. "I'm going to Los Angeles."

This made them laugh even harder. "Oh, bullshit. You've been saying that for years."

It was a slap in the face. No one had really called me out like that before. I'd been saying I was moving to California for four years by this time, and everyone always just nodded and smiled. Now here they were telling me I was full of shit. Delusional. Worst of all, that I was going to stay in Toledo forever.

"Fuck you," I said. "I'm leaving."

"Right, Khalil. When? When are you leaving?"

"I'm fucking leaving tomorrow."

"You aren't going anywhere, man." It was my friend talking but the voice came from every negative moment in my life. It came from my worst fears.

"I'm leaving tomorrow," I repeated. "Who's going with me?"

"Sure, why not?" they said out of drunkenness and mockery. "Let's all go!"

I woke up the next morning at my mother's apartment with the worst hangover of my life. I didn't remember how I got there or anything about driving back from Detroit. But I *did* remember standing on that car saying I was moving to California tomorrow. No, now it was *today*.

I lay there with my stomach churning and head throbbing. The thought of dragging myself into whatever shitty job I had to do that day was unbearable. Waiting tables, hauling sheetrock; even selling pot had zero appeal.

I made it into the shower and brushed my teeth a few times. I thought that might make me feel a little better, but it didn't. I grabbed the few things I kept at my mom's place and packed it all in the car. I was 21 with $600 to my name, no map, and no plan. Was I actually doing it? Was anyone going to stop me, beg me not to go? I needed someone to, because otherwise I was driving to California. I was too proud and stubborn to back down after the previous night.

My father got to work every day at 5:00 p.m. on the dot. He was never late. I was in the parking lot when he pulled in and walked past my car.

I beeped my horn and rolled my window down.

He stopped. "Yeah?"

"I'm moving to California."

He took it all in for a moment, looking into my car. I had strategically positioned my backpack full of clothes and my pillow so that he could clearly see them in the back window.

"Good luck."

Then he walked away.

I couldn't believe it. I shouldn't have been surprised at all but some part of me still hoped he would turn into the dad I needed. I drove with tears in my eyes to the 70-80 Turnpike and pulled onto the westbound ramp. I couldn't stop crying, and I sure as hell couldn't stop driving. I knew if I stopped I'd never leave Toledo.

I chain-smoked cigarettes and pounded Diet Cokes to stay awake until late that night. I almost made it across Illinois before I had to stop and sleep. I was emotionally exhausted and still extremely hungover. I got a room at a Motel 6, turned the TV on, and collapsed onto the bed.

The channel was showing a Burt Reynolds movie. He'd decided to kill himself by chaining a huge brick to his leg and jumping into the ocean. At the last minute, though, he changed his mind. That's the last thing I remember until I woke up with smoke in the room. My eyes burned. The smell of melting plastic made me gag. Frank Sinatra's "My Way" came from the TV, which was on fire. The screen flickered and flames jumped out of the back. I rubbed my eyes and tried to make sense of it all.

I was still half-asleep when I called the front desk. "Hi. My TV is on fire."

"Very funny." They hung up. I called back and the desk attendant said, "You goddam kids, you stop—"

"My fucking room is on fire!" I screamed.

The next thing I knew someone was pounding on my door. The desk attendant barged in with a fire extinguisher and doused the TV. He was pissed, like I'd intentionally set the damn thing on fire. The hallway was full of people trying to figure out what was going on. I was exhausted, dehydrated, and delirious. This all felt like some drug-induced nightmare. Is this what happened to everyone who left Toledo?

The motel put me in another room and I passed out again until noon the next day. When I woke up, I didn't know where I was. The room had vinyl drapes tainted yellow from cigarette smoke, the acoustic cottage cheese ceiling had a multitude of strange, various colored stains—I didn't want to guess from what—and the air smelled stale and cheap. And then it all came crashing back.

"Oh my God," I said, "what the fuck did I do? What was I thinking? This is crazy!"

No one was there to tell me it would be okay. That everything would be fine. It was just me.

"What am I going to do?"

I got a giant coffee from McDonald's and got back on the Turnpike.

West.

It was like there was an anchor connecting me back to Toledo, to my past, and the farther I drove the harder it tried to pull me back. But I kept going and a funny thing happened. As I was swept along in the flow of traffic, I felt a little tickle in my stomach. Excitement was starting to override the fear. Momentum was getting stronger than the anchor.

I didn't even listen to music for most of the car ride. I fell into a semi-meditative state from the constant blur of the lines on the road and a feeling of solitude I'd never felt before. I'd always sought one distraction or another—alcohol, drugs, drama, girls—to keep me from feeling alone and isolated, but as I drove west I actually enjoyed my own company for the first time. I could finally find out who the hell I was outside of my fucked-up little existence in Toledo.

When I did listen to music it was a mixtape I'd made—Big Audio Dynamite, Killing Joke, Jane's Addiction, The Pixies, etc. I kept replaying "Rush" by Big Audio Dynamite:

If I had my time again
I would do it all the same
And not change a single thing
Even when I was to blame
For the heartache and the pain
That I caused throughout my years
How I loved to be your man
Through the laughter and the tears
Situation no win
Rush for the change of atmosphere
I can't go on so I give in
Gotta get myself right outta here

I rolled the windows down and cranked up the volume. It was October and the scenery across the country was absolutely breathtaking. Whenever I stopped for food or gas, no one gave me dirty looks or whispered to one other about how I was that "bad kid." The people I met sensed my enthusiasm, my passion, and my purpose. They smiled at me. I was a man on a mission and it was apparent to everyone.

When I wanted to revel a bit in the sadness of my situation I'd switch to "The Last Night on Maudlin Street" by The Smiths:

> *...and as we spend the last night*
> *on Maudlin Street, I say*
> *"goodbye house-forever!"*
> *I never stole a happy hour*
> *around here*

I'd sing along and cry, but not in the same way I had when my father had said "good luck" and had walked away. This was a good cry. A release. Shedding all the isolation and depression of 21 miserable years.

I was fooling myself.

Sure, I was leaving Toledo and the people who had hurt me behind, but all the other baggage came along for the ride—a crazy, chaotic ride that would cost me everything.

CHAPTER THREE

IT WAS WELL PAST MIDNIGHT AS I CLOSED IN ON THE FINAL hundred mile stretch to Los Angeles. I can't remember what hill, mountain, or pass it was (I think it was somewhere near Pomona), but I will never forget the feeling I had as I drove over it and began to descend. Sometimes the universe, or God, plays DJ in your life. This was one of those moments. "Mountain Song" by Jane's Addiction came on. I cranked it up to full volume as I stared out at the vastness of all of those lights, all of those tens of millions of lights, twinkling. I couldn't believe it; I couldn't believe a city was that big. I kept rewinding the song and playing it over and over, screaming the lyrics as loudly as I could, with all the windows down. I chain-smoked cigarettes and had goosebumps all over my body. My face hurt from smiling.

I've arrived, motherfucker. I am here. Now. I am here now.

I slept in my car that first night, somewhere near USC. The next day I reached out to my friend Kenny, the art student who'd invited me to visit him when I had been 17. He said "Sure, come on over," but he sounded weird. When I got there he acted even more awkward and nervous.

This went on for two days until I finally said, "Hey, man, what's up? You said I could come stay with you any time, but I'm getting the feeling you don't want me around."

He hesitated. "Amanda is coming here."

"What the hell?" Amanda was one of my ex-girlfriends. "Why would you tell her I'm here?"

"No," Kenny said, "she's coming here for me. Not for you."

Ouch.

Amanda showed up and then shit *really* got weird. She and Kenny spent the whole time locked in his room while I sat around wondering if I'd made a huge mistake leaving Toledo. Kenny's roommate, Dean, must have felt bad for me. "Dude, come up and hang with me in the loft."

"You sure?"

"Of course. Come on."

And with that small act of kindness, my life on the West Coast began.

✳ ✳ ✳

During my first year and a half in California, we had: the LA riots; one of the worst wildfires in the history of Malibu, with almost 17,000 acres burned; a massive earthquake that collapsed entire stretches of the freeway; *and* an El Niño, with the mudslides and flooding that came along with it. Ohio was boring as hell but safe—the worst we ever got was a blizzard and an occasional tornado. I was starting to wonder if this whole California thing was just one big, bad idea.

I rented a room in the Santa Monica Canyon for $500 a month. I'd been hired as a manager at a restaurant on

Fifteenth and Montana, so money wasn't a problem. The room was in this rickety, ancient mansion that had been picked up from beachfront property and moved to Entrada Drive. It was part of an estate that William Randolph Hearst had built for his girlfriend, Marion Davies. The house is a historic landmark now, but in the early '90s it was a complete shit hole and my room was by far the shittiest. *But,* it had the only 180-degree ocean view in the entire house and I took great pride in fixing it up.

The house was full of these eccentric people who defined California for me: a gorgeous, 5'11" blonde girl who was going to school at UCLA; a professional women's volleyball player; a struggling screenwriter; a wannabe producer. And it was two blocks from the beach. I could finally put my feet in the sand and watch the ocean.

Maybe I *was* gonna be okay after all.

Though there were periods of sobriety, every now and then I would join my housemates for some cocktails and a joint. I'd end up overdoing it (shocking, I know) and puking, blacking out, or both.

A few months after moving in I called my ex-girlfriend Claudia who was a student at the University of Michigan. I told her I missed her and loved her, and begged her to come see me. She ended up dropping out of U of M and moving to California to live with me.

It was a disaster from day one. We fought constantly. I knew this would happen even before she arrived, but my fear of being alone trumped my better judgment.

I got fired from the restaurant. One good thing that came from my father was a tremendous work ethic and attention to detail, and I told the owner that his staff was drinking the really expensive wine and that the waiters were overcharging people's checks by as much as $100 sometimes. I thought for sure he'd get pissed and fire people, but instead he got pissed and fired me. My Midwest naïveté left me oblivious to the fact that everyone who worked there, including the owner, was dealing cocaine out of the restaurant and couldn't care less about the expensive wine. And in hindsight, it made perfect sense why people's checks were being overcharged by $100.

Claudia and I needed a change of scenery. The volleyball player had moved to Malibu and needed roommates, so we relocated there and shared an apartment with her. Now I just needed to figure out a way to pay rent.

By this point I'd suspected I might be a bad employee. Not because I was lazy or dishonest—just the opposite. I couldn't keep my mouth shut when I saw somebody doing something the wrong way or doing something stupid, and it always caused friction with my co-workers and bosses. So I decided to try being my own boss.

One thing I'd always been proud of and good at was keeping my car clean. Even when my personal life was a disaster, my car was immaculate. I knew about all the different cleaning chemicals and how to get tires, upholstery, and trim work all looking brand new. Malibu was full of Porsches, Ferraris, and Lamborghinis, and I knew there was money to be made if someone was willing to do the work. So I printed flyers and started going door-to-door offering automotive detailing services.

I got very few callbacks and people in Malibu did *not* like me knocking on their doors asking if I could wash their cars. Once in a while, I'd get someone who was exceptionally nice, or perhaps just lonely, who would say yes, sometimes even inviting me in for lunch, but it was nowhere near enough to pay the bills. Going door to door was a bust, and I definitely wasn't getting any responses back from the flyers that I left on people's windshields.

One day, I was driving down Santa Monica Boulevard and saw a Porsche dealership. I thought, *Why not go to the source?* I went inside and gave them my whole spiel about how I was the owner of AutoNanny, the best detailing business in Los Angeles, and possibly the entire West Coast, and offered my services to them. They sent me back to talk to the service manager, Lodi. I started my pitch again and he cut me off.

"Do you have a place?" he asked.

What the hell? I was wearing my best clothes—khaki pants, collared shirt, penny loafers—and this dude thinks I'm homeless? "Yeah, of course I have a place."

"Where?"

I gave him the address of my apartment.

He frowned. "That's strange. I've never heard of it."

I was confused. Why would he need to see my apartment? In retrospect, he obviously wanted to know if I had a detailing shop, a place where the cars would be safe and locked up, and I'd just unknowingly bullshitted my way into convincing him I did.

Lodi tossed me a set of keys and pointed to a brand new Carrera 4 Porsche. "Take this for the night and bring it back tomorrow."

I was shocked. I raced home and picked up Claudia so she could drive my car back while I drove the Porsche. Then I detailed the hell out of that thing. It was cleaner than when it rolled off the showroom floor. I took it back to Lodi the next day and he barely glanced at it.

"How much?" he asked.

I knew the smart thing to do was give him a high number so he could work me down a bit. "$39.95," I said.

He laughed. "Why don't we make it $100?"

"Okay, $100 is good." I almost fainted.

He wrote me a check and tossed me another set of keys. Within a short time I was earning $125, $150, even $225 per car. Then Lodi recommended me to the BMW dealership. They didn't need me at the time, but a few months later the service manager called.

"Are you still detailing cars? I have a client in Bel Air who needs their car detailed. Can you go up there and do it?"

"Of course I can," I said. "That's what I do."

He gave me the address and I drove up into the hills of Bel Air, with all these huge majestic trees and giant hedges framing the huge estates. It was landscaping like I'd never seen before. These people weren't rich, they were *wealthy*. Every driveway had a massive gate and security cameras. I found the house and a young man named Tim let me in. It struck me as odd that the entire staff was made up of young gay men, but I was here to do a job and I didn't really care. I detailed the car, a blue 325i BMW, and when I was finished, Tim asked if he could mail me a check.

"Mail it? No, I did the work. I need you to give me a check."

For some reason this flustered Tim, but he cut me a check and I quickly left before I did anything to ruin it.

Five days later Tim called me. "Larry wants his car detailed again."

"But I just detailed it," I said.

"Well, he wants it done again. Can you please come up?"

"Listen man, you're only supposed to detail a car three times a year, maybe four. But if he wants it done again, yeah, I'll come up." I detailed the car again, feeling guilty because it barely had any dust on it, let alone dirt.

When I was done Tim asked me, "Can we mail you a check this time? Please. It's a lot easier for the estate accounting."

I was so confused. Why couldn't they just write a goddam check?

Then he said, "Also, if you could come up every week and detail all the cars, that would be great."

Every week? I was confident they were all on drugs, but I didn't want to blow the opportunity. And who was I to judge, anyway? "Yeah, sure, mail me a check and I'll be back next week."

When the first check arrived it came from some accounting firm in Beverly Hills and it had a guy's name on it that sounded very Jewish. None of these guys looked Jewish to me, not even remotely. Why were all these crazy gay guys wanting their cars detailed so much? But the check cleared. That's all I cared about.

After a few weeks Tim asked if I could detail the motorcycles, too. These guys were insane. The motorcycles, one of which was named "Purple Passion," looked like they'd never even been ridden. He took me to the garage and I got to work. After a while one of the staff members came in. He was clearly different from the others. For starters, he was definitely not gay. He was disheveled, smoking, and wearing a white t-shirt with yellow armpit stains. He didn't look like any of the other guys running around the place. He watched me work for a while, asked a few questions, then walked over to the refrigerator and opened it.

"Hey, man," I said, "what are you doing?"

He glared at me. "I'm getting a Coca-Cola."

"No, no, sorry man."

"What are you talking about?" he asked.

"Look," I said, "I'm working out here. This is my area. I'm responsible for this area. And I'm sorry but you can't have a Coke. I'm gonna take my lunch break soon and I can grab you one from the store."

He shut the refrigerator and looked at me for a couple of beats too long, like he was thinking about starting a fight or something. Then he laughed and went back into the house. I was pissed because I noticed that he had taken a Coke. On my lunch break, I grabbed an extra Coke from the market and carefully replaced it.

That night I got a call from Tim. "Larry wants to hire you full time."

"Who's Larry?" I said. "The dude that mails the checks?"

"No," Tim said, very patiently, "that's the accountant. Larry lives here. He wants you to be the houseboy."

"No, I'm sorry. I have my own business to run."

"Well, can you just do it temporarily? Our houseboy just moved back to Sri Lanka and we need somebody right away."

"Tim, I'm too busy."

He said, "We will pay you $800 a week."

I fumbled and dropped the phone. This was 1993 and $800 a week was a fortune to me. I took the job. I detailed cars and did whatever else needed doing for this Larry guy, whoever the hell he was. About two weeks after I started I was walking across the yard and the front door opened. That had never happened before while I was there. A little white dog came tearing out and ran up to me. I knelt down to pet it and when I looked up, Elizabeth Taylor was standing in front of me.

"Hello," she said.

I struggled to speak. She was unbelievably beautiful and elegant. She looked like a work of art. I finally managed to squeak, "Hello."

She knew the effect she'd had on me. She gave a small smile, called the dog back, and went inside.

I ran around back and found Tim. "This is Elizabeth Taylor's house?!"

"Yeah, lower your voice," he chuckled. "Of course it is."

"Why didn't you tell me?"

He frowned. "We assumed you knew. Don't you know who Larry is? Larry Fortensky?"

"I'm from Ohio! I don't know who anybody is!"

This was about to change in a big way.

* * *

I was still working for Elizabeth Taylor when word started getting around about how well I treated her cars and property. Pretty soon I was taking care of an entire airplane hangar full of cars that belonged to Slash from Gun N' Roses, which also led me to detailing cars for Axl Rose at his house in Malibu. It was still 1993 and they were the biggest band in the world. Axl was a rock star and he played the part to a T—pretty distant and incredibly hot and cold—but I'm not blaming him. As I said, he was the lead singer for the biggest band in the world and I was just the guy who washed his cars.

But Slash was different. I kept thinking he was confusing me with somebody else, somebody he knew, like an invited guest or something. He would be excited when I got there and always invited me into the house, asked me if I was hungry, and offered me a drink. And he had all these snakes—I don't mean like 5 or 10, I mean like 100. Literally. He had snakes everywhere and he loved showing them off. One day he was particularly excited and he said, "Come here, I gotta show you something."

He told me to sit down. He walked over and opened up a door and a giant cat came walking out. Not "cat" as in "house cat"—I mean "big fucking cat" as in "jungle cat." I'm pretty sure it was a cougar. It went right for me. It jumped on me with its two front paws and knocked me to the ground and began licking my face.

Slash quickly jumped up and pulled it off of me.

"I don't mind, man," I said.

"No, no, it's his tongue," he said. "If he keeps licking your forehead like that, he'll peel it right off your skull. His teeth are capped and he's declawed, but his tongue is so powerful, he could lick your face off in 20 seconds."

Around this time I was also referred to Jeff Bridges. He lived on the hill above my first rental in the Santa Monica Canyon and would call every now and then for odd jobs that needed doing, like clearing brush off a slope or changing a light bulb. He was one of the nicest, most amazing human beings I'd ever met. He was good to me, so kind, and would always come out and talk to me while I worked. He never failed to offer me a beer and always told me to go enjoy the pool house and go for a swim. There was something so different about him, so human and real. I was so upset when he decided to move to Santa Barbara.

Meanwhile, my relationship with Claudia took a sharp

turn. She went back to Ohio to visit her parents and before she got back, she called to tell me that her parents were very upset that she was living with someone out of wedlock, although I'm gonna go out on a limb and say it had more to do with me than the institution of marriage because by then we had already gotten engaged. They had presented her with a proposition: if she moved out, not only would they pay for her schooling, but pay all of her bills and pay off her debt as well. She was going to accept their offer.

I was furious. "Fuck you! We're supposed to get married!"

I hung up the phone. Over the next week, someone back in Ohio finally told on me— I think maybe her younger sister. When I was living in Ohio, everybody was scared of me and nobody dared tell Claudia anything, but now that I was long gone and it was common knowledge that I had slept with half the girls in that town while we were dating, I'm sure she got more than an earful about my escapades. When she got back to California, she didn't call; she just showed up at our apartment. She walked in, grabbed the vacuum cleaner, and threw it across the room at me. It hit me in the head. She jumped on me and pinned me down to the floor. She started kicking me. She even spit on me. Needless to say, Claudia moved out immediately.

* * *

So here I was, living in the twilight zone, working for rock stars and movie stars. I probably should have seen it coming. Working for all those wealthy people in Bel Air, Beverly Hills, and Malibu, it was only a matter of time before somebody asked me to score something for them. Not anyone I've mentioned; no one gets thrown under the bus here but me. Maybe I just had the look of someone who knew how to get shit. These people were used to snapping their fingers and getting what they wanted. So they asked, and I said yes.

A friend introduced me to some guys from Humboldt and Marin counties and I started driving up there to pick up pounds of marijuana. I paid $4,000 per pound and I'd break it down into ounces and sell them for $600. It was a hell of a lot easier than detailing cars and quite a bit more exciting as well. I quickly became disenchanted with real work and saw the massive potential of selling pot full-time. This wasn't like selling Mexican dirt weed in Toledo. This was the premium shit, as good as it gets. I couldn't buy enough of it. The moment I got it back to Malibu, it was gone.

I made a lot of money in a very short period of time.

Man, if my friends could see me now!

Then it hit me: it was impossible to get good weed in Ohio. I bought as much as I could and packed it into the trunk so I could drive back to Ohio and make a fortune.

A friend of mine from Toledo named Brian went with me. He was in California for law school at the time, which we both thought was pretty ironic. I drove the first 31 hours straight, jacked up on coffee and Diet Coke. When I started to nod off, I told Brian to switch with me. "Stay in the right lane, keep the cruise control at 60. Do *not* go over 60. Got it?"

"Got it," Brian said.

"Brian, I'm serious. Do not go over 60!"

"I won't, I won't" he said. "Though the speed limit *is* 65."

"Brian, just fucking listen to me. Do not go over 60."

"Okay, okay," he agreed.

I leaned the seat back, shut my eyes, and fell asleep. Not

even 10 minutes had passed when I heard Brian say "Oh shit."
I didn't open my eyes. I didn't need to. I knew what it was.
"Shit, what?" I asked sarcastically.

"I think we're getting pulled over," Brian said.

"Why would we get pulled over, Brian?"

"Well, I'm going like one mile an hour over the speed limit. I'm going 66."

My entire life flashed before my eyes, which were now clenched shut. We were in a little town called Vega near Amarillo, Texas, driving a rented car with California plates through a dry county and I had hair down past my shoulders. I knew we were screwed. The cops performed an illegal search and seizure. Brian was sobbing and lamenting about how his life was over. I honestly didn't see the big deal. It was just pot for God's sake! Clearly, I had never been to Texas.

I felt bad for Brian.

"Look, man," I said, "just bail me out and get me an attorney. Do that, and I'll sign a confession right now saying this is all on me."

Brian couldn't believe it. "Dude, really? Are you sure?"

"Yeah. Just get me an attorney, pay the fucking fines, and get me outta this shit!"

As I sat in that tiny room, waiting for the "bad" cop to bring me pen and paper, the "good" cop began nervously talking to me.

"Are you a singer?" he asked in his heavy Southern drawl.

I just stared at the ground.

"You remind me of that Jim Morrison fella'. I was down there in Jamaica back when I was in college on spring break. I kept listening to all that reggae music. I was so drunk and happy, hell I was jackin' off all over myself."

I suppose I should've laughed or something. This guy was bored out of his mind and hated his fucking life and was just trying to make conversation with me.

I signed a confession taking complete responsibility for the whole thing. And Brian, well, what do you think Brian did? Brian disappeared, never to be heard from again. Suddenly I was facing 7 to 10 years in prison with no one to help me. Who was I supposed to call, Elizabeth Taylor?

Well, somebody *was* looking out for me. I called Dean Carr, Kenny's roommate who had been so kind to me when I'd first moved to Los Angeles. Dean called his friend Stinky. Stinky was a low-end pot dealer, but he made his real money from computers. No one knew how to work on computers back then, but he was an expert. His real name was Chris but we never called him that—it was always "Stinky" or "Chris that never shuts the fuck up." Stinky was the dealer and computer technician for a very high-profile attorney in Palm Springs named Nick and he told Nick about my situation. Nick was a Vietnam vet, former Special Forces and Secret Service who was wheelchair-bound due to exposure to Agent Orange. He called the prosecuting attorney and read him the Riot Act over the illegal search and overall mishandling of the case. "You're going to cut this boy a deal," he said.

"Not a chance in hell," the prosecutor said. "He's doing 7 to 10. We're going to make an example out of him."

"You're going to cut this kid a deal," Nick said, "or I'm going to come down there in my wheelchair and I'll put your little fucking town on the map."

"What kind of a deal are we talking about?"

"Probation," Nick said. "Nothing but probation."

"I'll see what I can do," the prosecutor said, and hung up

the phone.

My bail bondsman's name was Bob Honeycutt and ol' Bob Honeycutt was a real shit-kicker. Cowboy boots and a big ol' cowboy hat (sorta goes without saying) and he smoked Pall Mall cigarettes, filterless I might add, and he drove a big ol' Lincoln town car with the A/C blasting, windows rolled up, and chain-smoked the fuck out of those filterless Pall Malls. I mean, I smoked cigarettes, too, but Jesus Christ, this was disgusting. I couldn't believe he didn't roll down his windows. He never stopped smoking and he never stopped talking.

At some point during our trip from the airport to the courthouse, Bob gave me his best version of tough love. He pulled that big ol' Lincoln town car over on the side of the road, threw the car in park, and, with a filterless Pall Mall dangling from the corner of his mouth, looked me dead in the eyes and said, "Boy, if you was a couple of shades darker, you'd never see daylight again so you'd better get some goddam gratitude and appreciation for our lord Jesus Christ."

I wasn't so sure about the Jesus Christ part, but as I sat in the courtroom that day, I realized good ol' Bob was telling the truth. Every single person who got up in front of the judge was black and every single one of them was detained on the spot, handcuffed, and dragged away to prison. I don't mean *kind of sort of*, I don't mean *most*—every single goddam one of them, for committing the exact same crime that I had committed: trafficking narcotics.

It was finally my turn to approach the stand. The judge read through my charges and asked if I had anything to say for myself. In my best Ohio accent, I gave him a lengthy speech about how I got mixed up with the wrong crowd and I was so sorry and I would never do it again. I even worked up a couple crocodile tears. I bowed my head as I spoke and dared not make eye contact with the judge until the very end when I said I was sorry for the last time and begged for mercy.

He gave me five years deferred adjudicated probation for a fourth-degree felony. That meant if I didn't violate the probation over the next five years, the conviction would be dismissed by the state of Texas. Like it never happened. It took nearly 8 months to get the deal finalized and every day I was convinced I was going to federal prison for 10 years. Suddenly I was facing a life worse than staying in Ohio. I had nightmares about it most nights. When I was assured the deal was done and I had received probation in Texas, I wept with relief.

The problem was, I lived in California.

I paid the $7,000 fine (well, actually, a model I was dating at the time named Anna gave me the money to pay it) and tried to get my probation transferred to California, which did not have deferred adjudicated probation. So according to my adopted state, I am to this day a convicted felon.

When it was all over, I was broke and homeless. I saw no other option than to move back to Ohio. I moved back in with Nicole and Debbie, feeling like a complete, embarrassing failure. I was there about three months when Nicole's father, Gus, who'd given me my first real job when I'd been 12 years old, called and said to meet him at the restaurant that night at 10:30. It was a strange time to get together because his restaurant closed at 10:00, but I'd do anything for Gus. I walked into his office and when he was done he said, "Let's go for a ride."

He drove us to a pizza place on Monroe Street. We ordered a pie and while we chatted and ate, he kept looking at me with a really serious face, then he'd crack up.

"What?" I said.

He just kept looking at me and laughing. When we were done he reached into his pocket and pulled out a huge wad of cash. He slammed the whole thing down on the table between us and slid it toward me.

"This isn't a loan," he said.

"What is it?"

"Get out of here. Get the fuck out of here. Do you understand me?"

I was lost. "What? Why?"

"Listen to me. Take this fucking money, and you get the fuck out of here and don't ever come back. You don't owe me nothing. Do you understand me? Get the fuck out of here and don't ever come back. Don't ever turn around. Go say goodbye to Nicole and Debbie tomorrow and then you're gone."

"Okay," I said. It stung. I loved him. He was like a father to me. A large part of me wanted him to want me to stay, but another part of me knew he was right. I just didn't have the guts to go back to California and my out was that I didn't have the money to go back. But now, with thousands of dollars in my pocket, I had no excuse.

He wasn't angry with me. He wasn't one of the many in that town who thought I was bad news. He loved me. He knew if I stayed in Toledo, it would be nothing but trouble. And he didn't want me to end up like him. He'd gone to California when he'd been 19 and had made plans to become an actor. He'd loved California more than anything, but his mother had gotten sick and his father had been a bad alcoholic and he had to come home and take care of his ma. I'll love him forever for what he did for me.

So I went back to California and made some calls. I got a hold of Mark, Slash's mechanic, a raging alcoholic from Dorchester, Massachusetts. He felt sorry for me and let me sleep in the spare room where he kept his animals: snakes, lizards, birds, and a rabbit that didn't have a cage and shit everywhere. The birds always kicked piles of seed out of their cages. It was one of the filthiest places I'd ever seen, but it had a roof.

Most of my detailing customers had moved on long before, but Slash was generous enough to let me take care of his cars, so I had a little money. I'd go to McDonald's once a day to eat and spend hours there reading. *Siddhartha*, *Demian*, and *Narcissus and Goldmund* by Hermann Hesse. *The Fountainhead* and *Atlas Shrugged*. *Stranger in a Strange Land*. Emerson, Thoreau. Anything I could get my hands on. Anything I could read to escape, to get my mind off of how fucked up and unfair life was— my life, anyway. I didn't have anything else to do, and I was tired of being ignorant. I was a high school dropout and now I was a fucking felon, so I figured I might as well educate myself.

The Alchemist by Paulo Coelho had the biggest impact on me. It gave me hope when I had none. It felt like the characters were talking directly to me: "The secret of life, though, is to fall seven times and to get up eight times."

So I got up. Only to fall further and harder than before.

CHAPTER FOUR

I DECIDED TO START WORKING OUT BECAUSE I KNEW THAT it would help with my depression. I went around the city looking at different gyms. I went to Bally's, which was cheap but disgusting and made me feel poor. I remembered reading in some self-help book in a bookstore that if you want to succeed, you need to surround yourself with successful people. So I figured I would kill two birds with one stone. There was a really fancy gym at the Lowe's Hotel on Ocean Ave that I had passed by many times. I walked in and looked around at the most incredible gym I'd ever seen before. The guy at the front desk was super friendly and offered to show me around. All the machines were brand new and gleaming and even though there weren't that many people working out, everyone who was there looked rich, successful, and in great shape.

He took me to the locker rooms. They were sparkling clean and even smelled nice. He pointed out the sauna and steam room. Then he took me outside and showed me the pool, which was overlooking the Pacific Ocean. I just about fainted. I didn't even think it was possible for a gym to be this nice. It was more like a spa or resort.

When we walked back inside, he asked if I'd like to join.

"Are you kidding, man? Of course!"

And then I stopped myself. I'd forgotten to ask how much it was.

"It's only $200 down and $175 a month," he said.

My heart sunk. I felt defeated and embarrassed. Bally's was $30 a month. I thought maybe this place was gonna be $50. I was about to puff my chest out and say something stupid like, "Yeah, maybe I'll be back. I'm gonna go check out some other places first."

But the guy seemed so cool and friendly, so I just thought *fuck it* and I was honest.

"I'm sorry, man, I can't afford that."

"Oh, don't worry about it," he replied. "I can waive the initiation fee."

I laughed.

"No, man. I can't afford the monthly fee. Like not even close. I don't have a job right now."

To which he replied, "Do you want a job?"

"What?"

"Do you want a job?"

"Where?"

"Here. Do you want a job here? I can give you a job. It doesn't pay much. It's only $6 an hour, but you'll have a free membership. And if you sell memberships to people who come in, you'll make a commission of $200."

Here I was, at 26 years old, being offered the same hourly wage I had earned as a dishwasher back when I'd been 12. But it didn't matter because his response told me two things:

1) this guy really *was* cool because he was willing to sacrifice his $200 commission and allow me to sign up without paying the initiation fee and 2) with the added prospect of commissions, I was about to make some real money because although I knew that I didn't know much, I could sell space heaters in hell.

I began working out like crazy and using the sauna and steam room. I felt like a million dollars. Within a short period of time, I started training people. I sold memberships and got commissions and my starting rate for training people was $50 an hour. I was fucking rich! Or at least it sure felt that way. I randomly cold-called Anna, the model who I used to date. I hadn't seen her since she bailed me out of the whole Texas incident. But things were a lot different this time. Now *I* had money. It felt great being able to take her to dinners and spoil her. I soon had enough money saved up to get a place in Malibu and we moved in together. It was the cheapest apartment in the city, but it came with a key to the most coveted private beach. This time around, I paid for everything.

* * *

So now I'm living in Malibu, making a bunch of money, and dating this awesome model from Iceland. For a moment, it felt like things couldn't get any better. Then one night, when I was working a late shift behind the counter at the gym, this guy came in who was really dirty and reeked of cigarettes. He tossed me his keys to put behind the counter and I noticed that there was a valet ticket connected to them. I loved it. I thought, *How bold.* I looked at the car key and you could tell that it was for a Jeep Wrangler. Again, I thought, *How bold.*

Who valets a Jeep? I loved that this poor guy who was filthy and smelled like cigarettes was valeting his car and working out at a fancy gym.

Later that night, when I was closing up, he stopped by the counter on his way out and we struck up a conversation. He asked me where I was from and I said, "I'm from Ohio."

He started laughing, to which I snapped back, "Fuck you, man. The best people come from Ohio."

He started laughing even harder and said, "I know, I'm from Columbus."

Then we laughed together as I walked him to the door and locked it behind him.

The next time he came in, we had a really great conversation about life, Ohio and California, and the friends we had left behind. As he was leaving, he said, "Can I ask you a personal question?"

"Yeah, anything man."

And he said, "You seem like such a smart guy. What are you doing folding towels in a gym at your age?"

He could see that I was crushed by the question.

"I just got outta fucking jail, man—not really something to put on a résumé. This was the only job I could get."

And then he said something I found very funny, which I'll never forget.

He said, "Here, give me a piece of paper." He scribbled down a name and number. "This is my assistant's number. His name's Todd. Give him a call. I can get you some work."

What the fuck was he talking about? His assistant? Rich people get assistants. There was no fucking way this guy had an assistant.

He's full of shit. He stinks like cigarettes, has dirt under his fingernails, and drives a fucking Jeep.

The following day, curiosity overtook me and I dialed the number. Todd picked up on the first ring.

"Oh, hey man. Yeah, Sam told me you'd be calling. Do you want to come by the office?"

"Sure," I said, thinking, *What office?* I was nervous, so I went and I got Anna and we drove over to the address. It was on Abbott Kinney in Venice, an interesting little artsy street surrounded on both sides by incredibly dangerous neighborhoods, riddled with crime and drug dealing.

When we walked into the office, I was shocked. Everybody was so fucking cool. Everyone was dressed so cool and looked so cool. I had never been around people like that before— artsy and smart and successful. Sam wasn't there but I met with Todd. I couldn't help but ask: "I don't understand what's going on here. What the fuck does this guy do?"

Todd explained that Sam Bayer was a director.

"A director?" I laughed. "How is he a director? If he's a director, why is he always so dirty when he comes into the gym?"

Todd started cracking up uncontrollably. "He's always dirty because he's also a cinematographer and he's always rolling around on the floor, shooting a million feet of film, trying to get the perfect shot."

I had no idea what he was talking about, but he moved on and gave me a call sheet for the following day. I was about to be baptized into the world of production.

"Oh, and bring your girlfriend, too, if you want. Sam said he might have a spot for her."

The following day, we arrived at what I could only describe as a scene out of a war, a battlefield. There were people everywhere, hundreds of people. There were trailers and buses and vans and shuttles. And there was Sam, standing on the hillside, screaming bloody murder and directing everyone.

"What's this shoot for?" I asked one of the staff.

"It's a Diet Coke commercial."

I was blown away. Before I had time to process the whole scene, Sam saw me out of the corner of his eye and yelled "Hey, Kleo"—the Ohio pronunciation of my name—"come over here!"

He was smoking a cigarette and drinking coffee and clearly pretty fucking wound up. He gave me a bear hug and said, "What's up, man?"

"This is my girlfriend, Anna," I replied.

He immediately screamed at one of the crew members, "Get her into makeup! Let's try to put her in a shot!"

Anna was freaked out. I was freaked out. He told me to go have a seat and that we would catch up later. Three hours into shooting that morning, way the fuck out in Antelope Valley, Sam yelled, "Get the kid's girlfriend! Get the kid's girlfriend! Let's get her in the shot!"

It was a circus—I mean that literally. It was a fucking circus. There were clowns and animals and people running around and dust flying up everywhere. Sam was rolling around on the ground with a camera and I finally understood what Todd had meant. He shot from every different angle, yelling and screaming the whole time. It was fucking brilliant.

Anna came out in an old-fashioned dress and stood on the hill while Sam rolled around on the ground some more, then stood on a ladder, then sat in a chair, shooting her from every possible angle. I thought it was so cool of him to do that—I figured he felt sorry for us and he was trying to make us feel special.

Six weeks later, as I started work on my third job with Sam, we felt special alright. Someone in the production office told me that Anna had made the final cut of the commercial, which would be airing soon. After the first run alone, we cleared over $75,000 in residual checks. The commercial ran constantly after that.

*　*　*

Working with Sam was a fantasy and a whirlwind of an experience. He was the first real artist I ever got to spend time with and he loved me, which was an added bonus. They paid me a fortune, $250 a day plus per diem on most shoots. Sam was mostly famous for music videos. He revolutionized the entire industry with the first video he ever did, which was for a little unknown band named Nirvana. He did commercials too—lots of them—for the biggest brands in the world. He even stuck me in a Nike commercial and they Taft-Hartley'd me and I got my SAG card.

I got to meet everybody—The Rolling Stones, Smashing Pumpkins, Metallica. It was literally a dream come true. I'm not really sure what my title was. I suppose it was Director's Assistant. But definitely not Assistant Director—that involved real work. I more or less just hung out, ran errands, or drove Sam to and from the set.

Something funny happened between me and Anna during this time. When I was making six bucks an hour and struggling to pay all the bills, we had this incredible bond. But when I started making all kinds of money with Sam, I started to get nasty. I always knew that she was way out of my league. She was a 6'0" tall blonde haired, blue-eyed model from Iceland and I was a 5'8" nobody from Ohio. Guys would always ask me, "How in the fuck did you meet her?" Direct translation: "What is she doing with *you*?"

I was always scared she was gonna leave. Why wouldn't she? She never acted like she was gonna leave, but I couldn't shake the fear. The better things got for us—the more in love I fell with her—the bigger the fear grew. I started snapping at her constantly. Sometimes I got so mean I would say things like, "You should just fucking leave, I don't want you here anymore," just to see what she would do.

She couldn't believe what I was saying. *I* couldn't believe what I was saying. The words would be coming out of my mouth, but inside I was thinking the exact opposite. I wanted to say, "I'm so scared you're gonna leave," but what would come out was, "You're a fucking idiot. You should leave. I don't want to be in a relationship anymore."

I couldn't make any sense of it, but it started happening more and more. We would always make up afterwards and there would be great sex and all, but then a week later I would do it again. I guess it gave me some sort of sense of security when she would cry. It made me feel like she cared and she wasn't gonna leave. I fell deeper and deeper in love with her. And the deeper I fell, the more scared I got and the more we would fight.

I began drinking more and more, with a fervor that I had never had. I developed an arrogance at work that obviously in hindsight I regret to this day. Sam was so generous with me— always taking me out to Hama Sushi and Nobu—but I still bitched and moaned and complained about shit. I started showing up late for work and sometimes not showing up at all because I was too hungover. Eventually, I got fired.

* * *

One day, Anna came home with good news—she had booked a music video for Michael Jackson. I think it was a remix of "Blood on the Dance Floor." It played here in the States, but it wasn't that big of a deal. But in Europe, it was a whole other story. It was the #1 video overseas. Television and radio networks from her home country of Iceland began calling incessantly, asking her for interviews.

I told her that she should go back and visit, but she said no because money was tight. I had lost my job with Sam and we were burning though our savings at an escalated pace. I remembered the sad stories that she would tell me of all the kids who would make fun of her when she was little because she had bad skin and was so tall and gangly. I insisted that she go back and show them all what a big success she had become.

"What about the rent? What about the bills?"

"Don't worry about any of that shit. You should go home. You haven't seen your family in four years."

She finally became excited about the idea of going home to visit. All of a sudden we were getting along so great—better than we ever had before. I figured while she was gone, I could focus on getting work. With two weeks to go and neither of us working, we spent every waking moment together. We didn't really have money to go out so I cooked every meal for us, and took great pride in doing so. I put so much love and attention to detail into each dish. They were simple dishes—poor people's dishes, I suppose. Lots of eggs and lots of pasta with red sauce. But there was love in those dishes—love and honesty.

When the day came for her to leave for Iceland, she was incredibly nervous, which made me nervous, too. She spent a lot of time pacing back and forth and staring at the ground in the apartment. We left early for the airport. We were driving down Lincoln when Anna began to cry.

"Oh honey, don't cry. It's fine. You're gonna be back in two weeks. Everything's gonna be okay."

She cried a little harder. She missed me already. It was amazing and heartwarming to see how much she missed me.

"Don't worry about anything. I called Dean Carr and he said I could come work for him."

She kept crying. She squeezed my hand tightly. It felt so good that she was crying like this, that she missed me so much. We had been getting along so great and she loved me. And that fear, that horrible fear I'd had, it wasn't there because I knew now that she loved me.

"I love you," I said.

"I love you, too," she whimpered as she kissed my hand and squeezed it tighter.

When we got to the airport, the crying turned to sobbing. I started to get choked up, too. It was so beautiful. My heart felt like it was bursting. She was my girl. I loved her and she loved me. I was so proud of myself for sending her back to Iceland so she could show all those mean people who'd made fun of her as a kid what a success she was now. I could just picture it—her getting interviewed by all those television and radio stations. I was so excited.

We got out of the car and we kissed. And she squeezed

me extra tight.

"I love you," I said again.

"I love you, too," she said as she turned and walked away.

She couldn't look at me and say it because it was too painful for her because she was gonna be gone for two weeks and would miss me so much. It made me feel so good, seeing her upset like that.

The whole way home, I felt great. I felt proud. I felt safe. I thought about our future together. I thought about maybe even having kids some day, but not for a long time. When I got home I heated up some leftover pasta and decided to go to bed early because the next day I would go find work and get things set up for when she came back. As I was walking up the stairs to go to bed, I felt a sudden wave of panic. She hadn't left me her mom's number. *Fuck,* she had forgotten to leave me her mom's number. *Fuck.* I had specifically told her 20 times, "Make sure you write down your mother's number in Iceland."

Oh whatever, I'll get it tomorrow when she calls.

Tomorrow never came. Well, tomorrow came, but the tomorrow when she called never came. By mid-afternoon, I was freaking the fuck out. Maybe the flight had been delayed. Maybe she simply got caught up with family. I fell asleep on the floor next to the phone. I woke up at dawn, freezing cold and achy and stiff from sleeping on the floor.

What the fuck? Something was wrong with the phone. Something was definitely wrong with the phone. I kept unplugging it and plugging it back in. I kept making local calls to friends and asking them to call me back to make sure it worked. I kept turning the ringer up and turning the ringer down. I called the phone company three or four times, asking them to do test rings because something was wrong with my phone. Maybe it didn't accept international calls or something. Yes, it did, they assured me.

I asked the phone company for the information number for Iceland. I dialed the number and a woman with a very heavy Icelandic accent answered. I told her that I was looking for Anna Robertsdotter and that she was staying with her mother. She said there were many Robertsdotters, that it was a very common last name in Iceland. Everyone's name there is either -son or -dotter. It's not like the US.

"What is her mother's last name?" she asked.

"I don't know."

"Well then how do you expect me to help you find the number?"

"I don't know."

They would only allow me three names per phone call, so I just kept calling back and getting more numbers for anyone named Robertsdotter. There were thousands. It took nine days straight. I didn't eat. I would fall asleep here and there with the phone in my hand. I would cry and then go into fits of rage, back and forth, back and forth. On the ninth day, I randomly found someone who knew someone who knew someone who was friends with Anna's father and I got his number. I called and he answered. He gave me the number for Anna's mother's house. She answered on the second ring. Not the mother, but Anna.

I dropped the phone at first. Then I yelled, "What the fuck are you doing?!"

She hung up. I called back again. She answered.

"What the fuck are you doing? What the fuck happened?"

She hung up again. I called again.

"Anna, please wait. Don't hang up."

"What?"

"What do you mean *what?*"

"What do you want?

"I want to know what's going on. When are you coming home?"

"I'm not coming back. I don't love you anymore. Please don't call here ever again."

And she hung up the phone. I called back over and over again, but no answer. Sometimes someone would answer and then just hang up on me. After a few minutes of this, I gave up.

I saw flashing lights. I looked up and a freight train of anguish, pain, fear, and abandonment hit me head-on and destroyed me. It shattered me into a thousand pieces. I died. I curled into a ball and I died. I lay on the floor, a puddle of putrid water, stagnant and rotting.

I can't even say that I was crying—I don't know what the sounds were. They were guttural, visceral, and horrid. Moans, groans, and shrieks. I sobbed and sobbed all through the night. I began to dry heave. I started to hyperventilate and then dry heave some more. I don't know how long it lasted—days, I suppose. Maybe a week. I was starving and my mouth was acidic and tasted like poison.

When I finally went out to buy groceries and cigarettes, the neighbors shot me weird looks or simply averted their gaze. They must have heard me. I hated myself and wanted to die and if I hadn't been convinced that I would spend all of eternity burning in hell, I would have done something about it. I would never trust again. I would never love again. I would never live again. Once again, darkness had overcome my soul and I willingly surrendered. I offered it up as a gift. And the door was opened wide for addiction to take the reigns.

✳ ✳ ✳

An old co-worker of mine at the gym, an Indian guy named Aaron, happened to be roommates with the manager of the band Porno for Pyros. His name was Roger. The lead singer of the band was Perry Farrell, who'd been the frontman for Jane's Addiction—one of my favorite bands—before they'd broken up.

I met Perry through Aaron and Roger, and Perry was very excited when he found out about my beach key. He loved surfing and started coming over. I typically went to John's Garden, the local sandwich shop, and grabbed us veggie sandwiches while he surfed because I didn't know how to surf and didn't want to embarrass myself out in the water. We would sit on the beach, eating the sandwiches, and Perry would talk and talk and talk. I never really understood what the fuck he was talking about. He would go on and on about birds and the planet and all kinds of other strange shit that I couldn't really follow. But I didn't care—I was talking to the guy who sang "Mountain Song," the anthem to my arrival in Los Angeles.

Soon after, I found out that Perry had decided to get Jane's Addiction back together. A couple weeks later he threw a party before the first big show of the *Relapse Tour*. I got to Aaron's house early and he, Roger, and I walked next door to Perry's. As soon as I walked through the door, there he was.

"Hey!" Perry said as he handed me a pill.

What do you do when the lead singer of your favorite band hands you a pill in his own house? You swallow it, and that's exactly what I did. It took about five minutes for the anxiety to kick in. I searched the house until I found Aaron.

I said, "Fuck, man! Perry gave me a pill. What was that?"

"Oh, *relax*," Aaron said. "It's ecstasy."

"No, no, no." I felt intense panic coming on and couldn't tell if it was the drugs or a panic attack.

"Hey, man. Calm down," Aaron said. "Take one of these."

He handed me a pill and I swallowed it, again. "Wait! What the fuck did you just give me?"

"That was a Swedish Quaalude. It'll calm you down."

"Fuck, man!" I shouted. "I can't just take these pills. I'm gonna freak out. I get panic attacks. I can't do psychedelics. I'll freak out!"

Aaron just looked at me and smiled. "You're not gonna freak out. You're gonna be fine. Just have a few beers."

So I did. Then I smoked a couple cigarettes. Everyone started getting really excited because it was time to go to the concert. We jumped into one of the many limos parked outside and rode into downtown LA to the Grand Olympic Auditorium. Perry was due onstage as soon as we arrived, and the rest of us grabbed our VIP passes and headed out into the arena.

It was pitch black. The low-pitched sounds of a didgeridoo and scratching guitar strings drowned out the screaming fans. Then there was an explosion of light and sound and the crowd went insane. The pills hit me all at once. It felt sort of like going down a roller coaster. I tried to tense up and control it—I even held my breath a little—but it was too late. The drugs and music combined to create a state of euphoria like nothing I had ever felt in my life. An atom bomb of bliss. A baptism of massive, excessive, and unnatural amounts of dopamine and serotonin. Any fear that I had ever had of psychedelics and, more importantly, losing control while on psychedelics, vanished in that instant, never to return again. I felt powerful, invincible, immortal. This wasn't just ego shit from hanging out with a rock star in a limo full of strippers—no, this was something else. It was an ecstatic state of total and complete oneness with the universe.

I woke up alone the next day on Westward Beach in Malibu. I didn't remember how I got there. I was sweating profusely and had no shirt or shoes on. I wiped the sweat from my face with my hands and when I looked at them afterward, I saw that they were covered in eyeliner and makeup. It must have been smeared all over my face.

The first thought that entered my mind: "Shit, I've gotta get more of that ecstasy. I wonder if I can buy it in bulk."

I called Aaron and he told me that what I had taken the night before had been very special ecstasy—that it had been cut with heroin, made especially for Perry. I suppose that should have scared the shit out of me—I had just casually found out that I had done heroin for the first time in my life—but unfortunately it thrilled me and only added to the excitement and anticipation of getting more.

Within a couple days, I had one 100 pills and I started selling them. Having access to marijuana had made me useful to the rich and famous, but having access to ecstasy made me a goddam celebrity. I got invited to every party, quickly made what seemed like incredible friendships with B- and C-list actors, and collected a small arsenal of phone numbers from model/waitresses.

My new suppliers weren't like the hippies from Marin and Humboldt counties, some Trustafarian white kids with dreadlocks who followed The Dead. These were *real* drug dealers. I immediately ramped up from buying 100 to 1,000 hits of ecstasy at a time—these were called "boats." The purchasing process changed dramatically. I was used to walking into someone's house in an upper middle class, white suburban neighborhood, handing them cash after smoking a bong with them, and then getting a bag in return. This time, there was a series of phone calls and very specific instructions. The last one was: "Drive to this location and wait."

So I did.

Four men in dark grey wool hats and parkas came out of nowhere and surrounded the car. These were real professionals—all about business. Lucky for me. If they'd been amateurs they probably would have taken the $8,000 in cash I very naïvely handed them and either left or killed me. No one would have known or cared. But they took the money and came back with the 1,000 pills because they knew I'd be back with more money.

"Don't ever bring us twenties again."

I laughed nervously, which was stupid. An idiotic move like that could have easily gotten me shot. I knew I should have been terrified, but it felt very glamorous.

I bought the pills for $8 apiece and sold them for $20-$30 each. I had a few other people selling for me, friends who wanted to make some extra cash, and the thousand pills went quickly, sometimes within a couple of hours if we hit a rave. We could honestly tell people how well they worked because the first thing I did after getting the "boat" was break a pill in half, swallow it, then crush the other half and snort it.

I became friends with a group of girls I sold to at all the raves, and one day one of them said her mom wanted to buy some ecstasy. I made the sale and wound up dating the girl, Jennifer. Things progressed very quickly, as relationships fueled by drugs often do. Her parents were concerned for our safety given our lifestyle and suggested I move in, which I did. Only in Malibu...

My drug use quickly escalated. I was taking massive amounts of ecstasy without eating or sleeping for days at a time. Then I'd crash. I'd wake up and think, *God, I feel like shit. What am I doing? I'm a drug dealer. I'm selling ecstasy at raves. This is disgusting.* That's when I'd try to clean up my act and find honest work...for a week or so. The money and the adrenaline rush from buying, selling, and using ecstasy was too enticing.

Eventually my company shifted to people who dealt harder stuff than the MDMA that I was peddling, like GHB and Ketamine, which is a medical-grade anesthesia. They told me and my friends that we could drive down to Tijuana and legally buy anything we wanted. Xanax, Valium, you name it. We were like kids in a candy store. We quickly made a routine out of buying cases of pills, stuffing them into tight leggings or knee-high athletic socks we wore under our jeans, and smuggling them over the border. This was pre-9/11 and, because we were American, the border agents never hassled us. Back home, we sold the pills for an 800% markup.

Smuggling the Ketamine was a different process. It came in vials of liquid from veterinarian supply stores. We bought cases of it at a time, cracked the vials open, and poured the clear liquid into water bottles. It worked like a charm.

Except for one time.

I was coming back into the country on a bus and they stopped me on the US side. The agent pulled me off the bus and pointed to my water bottle. "What's that?"

"Nothing," I said. It was pure GHB.

"Have a drink of it," he said.

"Sure." I opened it up and took a big chug, much bigger than I needed to just to make sure he was satisfied. The GHB started hitting me immediately but I kept my composure until he let me get back on the bus. I barely made it. By the time I staggered to my seat I had completely lost my shit, both literally and figuratively. I actually shit my pants. But I didn't get caught.

Soon after that my girlfriend Jennifer and I were back in Mexico buying a particularly large amount of Ketamine. I pulled out a huge wad of cash, peeled off half of it for the owner of the supply store, and stuck the rest in my pocket. I'd done business there before and we typically carried our stuff out the back to avoid crowds. This time the guy said, "Oh, you don't need to go out back. You can just go upstairs and my guys will help you."

How nice! I thought. *They're going to help us open all these vials and pour them into bottles.*

So Jennifer and I followed five of his guys upstairs and we started dumping the vials. At first the guys were helpful, then a couple of them quit working and started shifting around like they were waiting for something. I realized they were about to fuck us up. And this was Tijuana in 1999—these guys could kill us and throw us in a fucking dumpster and no one would care.

Something rose up inside of me that I had never felt before. I felt hot. My temples started throbbing. My fear quickly turned into rage as I slowly moved my hand under my shirt as if I had a gun. In slow motion, with murder in my eyes, I looked at each man. They stared. I stared harder. I dared not blink or look away. It seemed like an eternity and I could feel sweat begin to trickle down my back, but I didn't flinch. No words were spoken. There was just a general understanding that if they came near me, one of them, if not several, was going to lose his life.

They bought it. They started backing away and I threw all the Ketamine and water bottles into a bag, spilling a lot in the process, but I didn't care. I kept my hand under my shirt and stared the guys down while we backed out of the room and ran like hell.

We could have easily been killed. Unfortunately, this became a frequent theme in my life.

* * *

It was 1999 and raves were happening every weekend. My days were a blur of drugs, sex, and parties. We took ecstasy on Friday night and partied until Sunday morning, then popped a few Xanax and passed out until Monday evening. We got up to eat, then went right back to bed. I stayed relatively sober all week and then I'd do it all over again.

I felt untouchable. I'd get pulled over by the cops with massive amounts of drugs in my car and they'd let me go without a search. Had they found the drugs, with me being a convicted felon, I'd still be in prison today.

As the year went on, things began to darken. A bunch of us went to the first Coachella in October. By then I was taking ecstasy on Wednesday, sometimes even Tuesday, and staying awake until Sunday before passing out for two days.

I distinctly remember my friend David and I going to pick up Eden, a fun and rambunctious girl who we often partied with. A little girl answered the door. She stared at us with the biggest, bluest eyes I'd ever seen, looking straight into our souls, which I can't imagine was a pretty sight.

"Who are you?" she asked.

"I'm Khalil."

She shut the door in my face. Eden came to the door, apologized, and let us in. We waited for her in the living room while she finished getting ready. All the while that little girl kept looking at me with those big blue eyes, those innocent but all-knowing eyes. I squirmed in my seat, knowing that any trace of purity that I may have been born with was gone, and it was never coming back.

As we left, I jokingly nudged David and said, "I'm gonna marry that girl some day."

He laughed.

* * *

I laughed at anyone who suggested I was a drug addict—that I should slow down, take it easy. I assumed they were jealous of my glamorous lifestyle. But part of me, as small and quiet as that part was, knew I was a 28-year-old drug dealer and addict. That my life was not what I had planned when I left Toledo. But I justified it because it kept the depression and panic at bay, and because the partying had introduced me to three very talented musicians who invited me to join them as the lead singer.

Music had played a vital role in my life and survival up

to that point, and when I made music with these guys I was certain it was the reason I'd come to California. It was my calling. So any drugs and parties that came along with it were just part of the deal.

A couple of my new bandmates were into heroin—*real* heroin, not ecstasy cut with heroin. I avoided it at first. For some reason I had expected it to be this glamorous high, something only models and rock stars could pull off. But these guys were smoking it off tin foil and snorting it out of the bottom of a beer can. It smelled awful. But it didn't matter how gross it seemed—I knew it was only a matter of time before I tried it.

We were at a party at my friend Todd's house up in one of the canyons near Malibu. He threw epic parties, like mini-raves, and charged $10 a person to get in. This time there were a couple hundred people there. The music was blasting, everyone was high on ecstasy, and they all loved me because I was the one supplying it. Pretty much anything they wanted, I could get, and I always joked about getting heroin.

"Hey, let's get some H."

"When are we gonna do some heroin?"

I only did it for shock value. There was something about it that scared the shit out of me. I made my way to Todd's room, which was like a party within the party. It's where the coolest people would hang out. I was being my typical self, super high and holding court for all the girls and anyone else who'd pay attention to me. A group of guys showed up and wanted to get into the party but they didn't have any money. They were friends of the guys I played music with so I let them in and they followed me into Todd's room.

One of them asked, "You got any ecstasy?"

"Yeah, they're $20 apiece. But you obviously don't have any cash."

The guy said, "Well, do you wanna trade?"

"Do I wanna trade? Trade what?"

"Do you want some heroin?"

The room went quiet. "Do you want some or not?" he asked again.

"Yeah," I said. "Sure."

"Let me get a couple hits of ecstasy."

"Show me the heroin," I said.

He pulled out a tiny yellow balloon and tore it open with his teeth, revealing a black, gooey mass. He took an empty beer can and cut the bottom off, flipped it over, and put some of the heroin in it like it was a tiny frying pan. He held a lighter underneath to liquefy it, then asked for a pen. He pulled the top off and the ink tube out, then cut the barrel with a knife so it became a straw. And then he handed it to me.

I just stared at him. "What?"

"Here you go."

"What am I supposed to do with that? Drink it?"

He said, "Look, dude, this isn't fucking *Pulp Fiction*. This is the real deal. This is heroin. Do you want some or not?"

A bunch of people in the room laughed. I felt like I was back in Toledo with everybody waiting for me to back out of moving to California. I was trapped by my own big mouth and ego again.

"Yeah, yeah," I said. "Of course I do."

"Watch," he said, then snorted a bunch of the liquid up through the pen into his nose. "That's how you do it."

He held the pen out to me again.

I grabbed it and snorted the rest. A warm numbness immediately spread though my body as I slid down the wall behind me. It was a feeling of comfort, ease, and peace. I sat there slumped against the wall with the symphony of ecstasy, Ketamine, and heroin all playing at once.

As for the guys who gave the heroin to me, I didn't like them at all but you better believe I got their number. I wanted more. I loved the way it felt, but I also loved how much it freaked people out when I did it in front of them.

At the same time, I hated it. It smelled awful and made me vomit and constantly scratch my legs, arms, and nose until they were raw. When my girlfriend Jennifer asked me why I kept doing it, I'd laugh and say, "Because I'm a musician!"

The truth is, heroin gave me what I had always wanted: a childhood. My brain had become fried from all of the ecstasy, acid, Ketamine, GHB, mushrooms, etc. The levels of pleasure I was forcing upon my mid-brain with the chemical romance of all of these illicit substances was simply not sustainable. Heroin was different. With one inhalation, I felt peace and calm, no depression, no anxiety, no hunger, no pain, no *any-thing* really. I became insulated and protected, warm and calm, fearless. I wrote songs and poetry and spent most of my time fantasizing in a half-awake state of lucid dreaming.

With my newfound love affair with heroin, I didn't have time for the day-to-day drug dealing, but I did manage to pull off a couple of really big deals selling Ketamine whole-sale to a big rave promoter in Hollywood. With the arsenal of cash that brought me, I bought myself some John Paul Gaultier sunglasses and Chrome Hearts clothing and began walking around like I had a three-man entourage behind me at all times.

One night I was at the Malibu Inn watching a band play, high as a kite on heroin and ecstasy. I went outside to smoke a cigarette and there was an actor, let's call him James, sitting at a table with a bunch of girls. I had some girls with me as well, and he called me over.

"Hey, sit down."

I melted into a chair at his table, feeling euphoric from my chemical cocktail.

"You want a base hit?" he asked.

I had no idea what a base hit was but I wasn't going to embarrass myself. "Yeah, sure."

He handed me a glass pipe. I took a hit and the pipe hit me right back with an immediate, overwhelming rush. It felt like my heart was gonna explode, but not in a bad way. My ears started ringing. I grabbed onto the sides of the chair so I wouldn't be rocketed into space. There was something orgasmic about it. It was the strongest substance I had ever put in my body and there was no fucking mistake about it—it was wrong. It was dead wrong. It was like robbing-a-bank-and-getting-away-with-it wrong, but goddam did it feel good.

"Oh my God," I said.

It was crack cocaine. No one in Malibu called it "crack," though—that was for poor drug addicts in the inner city. Here it was called "freebase" (or "base"). Freebase is a smokable form of cocaine that became famous during the seventies by processing it with ether. We, on the other hand, were smoking cocaine processed with baking soda and water, also known as crack cocaine, but to ease our consciences, we always referred to it as freebase.

James smiled and invited me to come to a party at his friend's house. We all smoked crack until the sun came up.

Afterward I went to Jennifer's house. I couldn't believe what I'd done. I was on the verge of tears when I woke her up and told her, "I just smoked fucking crack all night. It was the most disgusting thing ever." I told her it was like sucking the devil's dick.

"I feel evil. I'm never, *ever* going to do that shit again."

I lasted two days.

I called James and went to his house with enough heroin to kill a small army. He had an ounce of crack already cooked up. We smoked it for three days straight. I was invincible. I felt like I could do anything. I don't know anything about basketball, but I was 100% certain that I could go try out for the Los Angeles Lakers and make the team if need be, regardless of the fact that I was 5'8". When we finally stopped, I felt dark, filthy, and disgusting again. It was scarier than anything I'd ever felt before. Worse than the feeling of being at a loved one's funeral. But I discovered that if I smoked massive amounts of heroin, it would counteract those feelings and eventually I just fell asleep.

The people around me saw the path I was on even though I couldn't. I had been smoking heroin every three hours for three months and now I was into crack. My friends tried to talk to me about it but I would laugh it off or call them out for being too weak to handle drugs the way I could.

Then one morning I got out of bed at the house I shared with Jennifer in Decker Canyon and I opened my drug drawer like I always did, pulled out my tin foil and straw, dropped some tar (heroin) in, and started smoking it. It was the norm for people to crash at our place after days of partying, and Jennifer's little sister Amy was sleeping on the couch. She woke up and watched me for a few minutes before I noticed she was awake.

"What are you doing?" she asked.

I kept smoking the tar. "What do you mean?"

"Why are you doing that now?"

"Huh? What do you mean?"

"It's 8:30 in the morning on a Sunday," Amy replied. "Why are you doing that?"

"What's the big deal? I'm just having a little bit. I feel hungover."

"Why don't you stop?"

"Because I don't want to," I said.

Amy said, "Will you stop for me?"

"I can stop any time I want."

"Any time?"

"Yes, Amy, of course. I can stop any time I want."

"Great," she said. "Then stop now."

She had challenged me and my ego wouldn't let me back down. I put the tin foil and straw away. "No problem."

She looked skeptical. "So you're gonna stop now? That's it?"

"Yeah, absolutely." I had watched *Trainspotting*. I could pull this off.

"Great," Amy said. "So what do we need to do?"

"I just need to get a hotel room. We'll drive down to Tijuana, get some Xanax and some Valium. And a gram of tar, just in case. I'll be fine."

I threw everything away. All the filthy, sticky pipes and lighters and straws. We went to Santa Monica and I bought one gram of heroin and gave it to Jennifer. She put it in the glove box and we started driving down to Tijuana.

Traffic was terrible and about three hours into the trip I started to feel sick. It was a weird, festering nausea that I'd never felt before. I didn't know what was going on. I thought I had the flu.

"You know what?" I said. "I need to stop and get a hotel. We can go to Tijuana tomorrow and get some pills."

We got a hotel room close to the border and I fell asleep until 10 o'clock that night. When I woke up, I exploded with vomit and diarrhea. I didn't even make it out of the bed. It was relentless. Jennifer and Amy kept giving me Gatorade and it came out immediately from one end or the other. This went on all night. I was covered head to toe in vomit and shit and I screamed all through the night. Jennifer and her sister shared the bed next to mine and had to listen to all of it. It must've looked and sounded like an exorcism. Amy couldn't stop crying.

I thought for sure I was going to die. I had no idea what was going on—I didn't realize this was withdrawal. I thought there was something seriously wrong with me—that I had contracted some fatal disease.

The next morning, the hotel room looked like a crime scene and the smell was unbearable. We grabbed our stuff and left, then drove across the street and checked into another hotel. In a brief moment of lucidity, I realized I'd seen something like this before. I had been buying heroin from a guy named Chris and I'd met him at a McDonald's. He'd had a friend with him, this really sweet kid named Hunter. I had been going to drive them to their dealer so they could buy me a gram.

Hunter had been shaking and looked green. He'd said, "Hang on."

He'd run over to the garbage can and thrown up.

"What's wrong with him?" I'd asked.

"Oh, he's fine," Chris had said. "He's just got the sickness."

"The sickness?" I'd asked. "What are you talking about?"

"He's dopesick," Chris had said. "He's in withdrawal. He'll be fine. He just needs some tar."

I kept thinking about that while I was in the hotel room writhing and shaking with goosebumps all over my body. Everything smelled terrible to me. I couldn't stop throwing up. My entire body hurt. I tried taking a shower but the water hitting my skin felt like fire burning me. It hurt no matter what the temperature was.

I didn't realize it at the time, but for the better part of three months I had been taking a powerful painkiller. I had replaced all of my natural dopamine with heroin and my body didn't know how to operate without it.

I was sobbing and vomiting as I told Jennifer, "I need to go to a hospital. I know where I need to go."

Long before I had turned into a full-blown drug addict, back when I was just detailing cars and selling pot, I'd met a guy up at Axl's house named Shannon. He was from Indiana, the next state over from Ohio, and we'd bonded over that. Shannon had just gotten a record deal with his band Blind Melon and he'd been happier, as he put it, than a "two dicked dog." We sort of stayed in contact, but not really, until one day I'd gotten a phone call from him and he'd told me that he was in rehab at a place called Exodus in Marina Del Rey. I'd gone to visit him a couple of times there. I knew I had to get to Exodus.

Jennifer and Amy drove me there and I told them to wait in the car. I didn't want to enter rehab—I just wanted the medication that would make the withdrawal symptoms stop. The hospital was a lockdown facility and, when a couple of nurses got buzzed through the back door, I sneaked in behind them.

I went right up to the front desk, still shaking and nauseous. "I need to get some medication. I think I'm gonna die."

The nurse said, "Okay, what's going on?"

"I just need to get some medication. I'm gonna die."

One of the male staffers said, "Wait a second. Where's your wristband?"

"What do you mean?" I replied.

"Who are you?" he asked.

"Oh, uh, um, I...I just need to get some medication."

They immediately called security. The guards dragged me toward the doors as I cried and shook uncontrollably. A doctor was walking out at the same time and I reached out to him. "Please help me. Will you please help me?"

His name was Dr. Waldman. He stopped the security guards and asked me, "What's wrong?"

I said, "I'm going through withdrawal and I'm gonna fucking die. Please help me. You helped my friend Shannon when he was here."

"Shannon who?" the doctor asked.

"Shannon Hoon," I replied.

"Do you have insurance?"

"No."

"Do you have any money?"

"No," I said. "Look, I'm a heroin addict. I need help. I've got a gram of heroin in the car, but I don't wanna do it because I don't wanna be sick like this again."

Dr. Waldman asked, "You have a gram of heroin in the car, but you're not doing it?"

"Yeah."

He looked at me suspiciously and said, "Show me."

I walked him out to the car, along with one of the male attendants named Nile. "Jennifer, give me the gram."

She gave me a confused look, then opened up the glove box and handed me the balloon. I handed it over to Nile. He opened it up, looked inside, and said, "I'll be damned. That's pretty impressive."

"Come with me," Dr. Waldman said. He then told Nile to go flush the balloon of heroin down the toilet.

He took me into his office, asked me some questions, and checked my vitals. "Look, you're just going through withdrawal. You're gonna be fine." He stuck a Clonidine patch on my shoulder and I immediately felt better. "Just keep this on for the next couple of days and drink lots of fluids. You're gonna get through this. You're gonna be fine."

He had me come back a week later for a full checkup. He even invited me to come to the weekly meetings they held there for people who had gone through the treatment program and for the people who were staying in their sober living. I never took him up on the offer. As many drug addicts like to say when they're in the midst of crisis, I was fine.

And I was fine.

For about a month.

❉ ❉ ❉

The acute portion of the heroin withdrawal lasted for five days. When I finally broke through I thought, *Fuck this! I'm done.* I repeated it in my head like a mantra.

Jennifer and I abandoned our house in Decker Canyon. We left our furniture, we left everything. We moved in with a friend named David who lived up another canyon in Malibu.

"You can stay here, but you can't get high," David said.

Jennifer said the same thing to me. "You can't get high, Khalil. Please don't get high anymore."

"I won't. I promise."

Even I believed it. I was done with drugs, done with being sick, done with all of it. It was the year 2000, a new millennium, and a new beginning.

Then one day my phone rang. It was a movie director I had scored heroin for a couple of times who I had taken a real liking to.

"Hey, man, can you get me some more of that stuff?" he asked.

"Yeah, sure." I thought nothing of it. I obviously wasn't going to do any myself. I had sworn it off 100 times that day alone. I drove to Santa Monica, bought a gram and a half, and took it over to his place. He had this massive house right on the beach, but I had never seen the inside of it because we had always done a handshake deal at the front gate. This time was different. He seemed genuinely happy to see me. He invited me in and I handed him the gram. Without even thinking about it, I kept the other half-gram in my pocket.

"Do you want some?" he asked me.

"No, no, I don't do it anymore."

"Are you sure?" By the end of the exchange, he had offered it to me five times.

Each time, I declined. "Yeah, I'm good. I don't do it anymore."

"Okay. Well, I'm right in the middle of a massage, but why don't you hang out? We can talk about your music afterwards."

"Yeah, sure," I said.

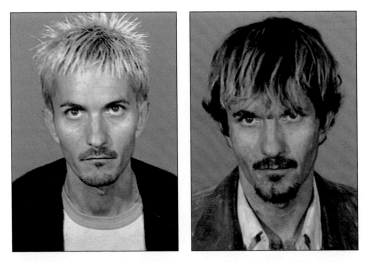

Left: The first of many mugshots (Charges: 1. Public intoxication 2. Under the influence of controlled substance). *Right:* LA County Jail mugshot (Charges: 1. Possession of controlled substance 2. Possession of drug paraphernalia)

Performing at the Malibu Inn. Notice the track marks on my hands and forearms.

Fell off stage performing in Santa Monica somewhere.

New Delhi, India. Doing service work and happier than I've ever been.

Touring Panama by helicopter.

Celebrating 10 years sober in Nicaragua!

Feeling victorious after an awesome hike in Red Rock Canyon.

Spartan Race 2014 with the incredible Crista, VP of Operations for SunLife Organics, and the rest of the SunLife team.

The Spartan Beast 2014. Crawling under razor wire with the voice of Steve Mihaylo ringing in my head: "Never, ever, ever give up."

Heading to Vegas on my friend's jet.

Living it up with my best friend from childhood, Teddy Papenhagen. The trip of a lifetime!

Khalil and Khen Rinpoche, Abbot of the Tashi Lhunpo Monastery in Bylakuppe India. I am blessed and honored to serve as a board member.

Hayley and I having a celebratory sundae at Hugo's Restaurant.

The fourth and newest SunLife Organics location at the Malibu Country Mart.

Of all the amazing things I've ever done, buying my mom this house is by far my greatest accomplishment.

By "massage," I'm pretty sure he meant "call girl," but who was I to judge? He told me to make myself at home, so I gave myself a tour of the enormous house, fascinated by the fact that he had this giant, beautiful pool and right beyond it was the ocean, with seemingly no separation between the two. I sat down on a big plush lounge chair and listened to the sound of the waves, but that sound was quickly overpowered by something else. The heroin began calling to me, to my soul. Like the sirens to the sailors, the heroin kept calling. This was spiritual warfare.

The heroin won.

I thought, *Ah, maybe I'll just have a little bit so he and I will get along. So he won't feel awkward doing it in front of me.*

I cooked it up, took one hit, and immediately vomited in his kitchen sink.

"Oh, fuck!"

I started to panic. I took another hit and threw up again, this time with even more force.

From the other end of the house, I heard the director's voice echo, "Hey, you okay?"

"Oh, yeah, I'm just coughing. I'm fine. *Cough cough.*" I thought if I smoked more tar, I would calm down and relax. So I smoked more and more. By the time he came back I was eight miles high. I got out of there as fast as I could with what was left of the half-gram in my pocket and went straight to David's house. Jennifer, David, and I talked for what seemed like an eternity. The entire time all I could think about was the contents of my pocket.

Jennifer finally went to bed, then David. I locked myself in the upstairs bathroom with some tin foil, a lighter, and a straw. I stayed up all night smoking every last bit of that tar, pausing only to throw up in the sink. And that was it. In a matter of hours I was not only right back to where I had left off, I was worse. Now I was lying about it to the people who loved me. I started getting up at the crack of dawn, while everyone else was still asleep, and driving to Santa Monica. I would get my fix, then drive back to David's to wake everybody up and make them breakfast.

I hid it well, even when my heroin addiction grew from $10 a day to $300 a day. The director would give me $1,000 to get him a gram, even though they only cost about $100, and I'd spend the rest on myself. I was back in the game. I started driving to downtown LA and buying grams for $30 and reselling them.

While my initial relationship with heroin had a brief honeymoon period before it went downhill, this time was like falling off a cliff into pure darkness. I quickly stopped caring if anyone knew I was using again. Jennifer was frustrated and angry, of course, but even she had no idea how bad it had gotten. She thought I was using recreationally and could stop again at any time. But that ship had sailed. It was as if the drug knew I was hooked for good now and could show its true form, its true destructive power.

As I said before, this was spiritual warfare. And that darkness was interested in one thing and one thing only: robbing me of my soul without my consent and destroying my life.

It was only a matter of time before Jennifer was using right along with me. She had been a drug addict from a very early age. She had started with the mild stuff when she'd been 12 and by 14 she'd been smoking meth. Her genetic predisposition toward addiction and my unrelenting pursuit of oblivion seemed to go hand-in-hand.

* * *

One day I met a much older guy named Manny at the Coffee Bean in Malibu. He could have been in his fifties, but he looked like he was pushing 70. We became pretty close and he would tell me stories about his days as a junkie back in New York when he was younger. And there *is* a difference between an addict and a junkie. I was an addict—addicted to ecstasy, GHB, Ketamine, heroin, and crack. But as bad as all that was, I wasn't a junkie. Junkies shoot up. I only *smoked* my tar. I managed to convince myself I had a sliver of my soul left because I'd never done that. This old guy had done it and kicked it. Although he still drank and smoked pot, he hadn't shot up in 23 years.

Every time we hung out I'd try to get him to smoke some heroin with me. He would laugh and say, "No, you're just wasting it. You're doing it the wrong way," which I wrote off as being arrogant and stupid.

Although he wouldn't smoke with me, Manny liked to party and be social. He had a recording studio in his house that we would hang out in and make music. So my new routine became: smoke a bunch of heroin and crack at Manny's place, make music, then make vows and pacts with Jennifer that we were getting off drugs for good.

We managed to get buprenorphine, a substance used for opioid detoxification and treatment, in glass ampules along with some intramuscular needles. We gave each other painful shots in the tricep, which hurt like hell but it eliminated any symptoms of withdrawal. However, it also eliminated the fear of getting back on heroin any time we felt like it. We didn't have to worry about getting dopesick, so why not?

One night I was having a particularly bad case of withdrawal symptoms, even on the buprenorphine. Jennifer and I started arguing because she wanted to go to a party at her sister's and I wanted her to stay with me.

"If you leave," I screamed, "I'm gonna go shoot heroin."

"Go ahead," she said, and left.

It was like my father saying "good luck" all over again. I drove up to that old ex-junkie Manny's house and told him, "You're always saying I'm wasting heroin the way I do it. I want to do it the right way. The real way. If you don't show me, I'll do it myself and probably end up dead."

"Whoa, slow down," he said. "You don't even have any needles."

"Oh, yes I do." I showed him the intramuscular needles from the buprenorphine.

He hesitated. "Okay, I just want to let you know something."

"Yeah, what?"

He looked me straight in the eye and said, "There's no Christmas for junkies."

"What the fuck is that supposed to mean? Is that supposed to scare me off?"

"Just remember I said that. There's no Christmas for junkies."

"I don't fucking care about Christmas. Can we just do this?" I held out one of my needles.

He shook his head and pushed my hand away. "Come with me."

I followed him downstairs to this toolbox that was always closed with a padlock on it. I'd always thought that was strange—he'd leave his wallet and cash sitting out with a bunch of drug addicts running around, but he kept a padlock on this old toolbox. He found the key on his keyring and opened the lid. The inside was full of hermetically sealed syringes, rubber tourniquets, and alcohol swabs.

"Why do you have all that shit?" I asked.

"Just in case."

"In case what?"

"The world ends," he said.

He unwrapped a needle and tied my arm off above the elbow with a tourniquet. Then he dropped some of my tar into a bent spoon and ran a lighter underneath until it liquefied. He rolled a small piece of cotton ball between his fingers and placed it into the liquid. The cotton sucked the heroin up like a sponge.

He stuck the needle into the cotton and eased the plunger back. The heroin drained out of the cotton ball and I watched intently as it was sucked into the barrel of the hypodermic. He set the spoon down and turned to me. I thought he was going to ask me if I was ready, if I was really serious about doing this, but he just slid the needle into the vein on the inside of my elbow. He tapped the barrel and pulled the plunger back even more and a beautiful plume of bright red blood, my blood, swirled into the dirty brown water inside the syringe. I was mesmerized.

"What are you doing?" I asked.

"Making sure it's registered."

"Oh."

Before I could finish that one syllable, he pushed the plunger in. Heat spread into my arm and I had the instant sensation of someone pouring warm milk down the back of my neck. It ran all the way down my body. None of the drugs I had done up to this point could touch this feeling.

I couldn't talk.

I couldn't move.

I felt nothing. There was no pain. There was no sadness. There was no anxiety. I'd never really felt the loving arms of my mother wrapped around me, but I imagine this is what it would have felt like. It felt like God himself was holding me in his embrace and that everything was going to be okay.

Everything was okay.

I would have to smoke a couple hundred dollars' worth of heroin to get even one tenth of that feeling. This was a tiny shot, less than $10 worth, and it lasted for hours. The old man was right: I'd been wasting it all along.

I smiled at him from my state of euphoria. It didn't bother me at all when he turned around, cooked up some more of my heroin, and shot himself up, too.

* * *

I stayed there with that old junkie for a couple of weeks, shooting up every few hours. He had tons of money he had inherited (old pre-car money), nowhere to go, and nothing to do. Jennifer eventually found me. Because she was an addict, too, she didn't see the bruises and track marks and scabs covering my arms—she only saw how fantastic I felt.

"I want to try it," she said.

"No fucking way," I said. "Not in a million years."

We fought about it for weeks. I knew what a bad idea it was for her, but she thought I just wanted it all for myself. Eventually, she wore me down. Within a month we were mixing cocaine with the heroin to make speedballs. We had finally reached the apex of oblivion. Nothing was more intense than speedballs—it was like going down a roller coaster and having an orgasm at the same time. It was the same feeling I'd had when I'd first tried ecstasy—times 1,000. Every time I shot up, I thought, *I want to feel like this for the rest of my life.*

And I didn't care how much more life I had, as long as I could spend it high on speedballs. I didn't give a fuck about anything anymore. Mixing heroin and cocaine is the most dangerous thing you can do in terms of drugs because you're speeding up and slowing down your heart at the same time. Many addicts die the first time they try a speedball. I knew that, but it only added to the excitement.

I stayed up for days at a time, shooting up every 20 to 30 minutes. I started driving into downtown LA to buy heroin and crack in large quantities. There were hotels down there, like the Cecil and the Rosslyn, that were essentially shooting galleries and crack houses. I would grab a room and stay for a few days, sometimes weeks. At first, I used sterilized needles right out of the package and threw them away after one use, but within a short period of time, I was re-using them over and over again. They became bent or broken, clogged with old blood, but I didn't care. I had to get that shit into my veins as fast as possible and nothing was going to stop me.

The objective of speedballs is to get high as fuck. The name of the game is to shoot right to death's door and wonder if it will open. The consistency and strength of the heroin and cocaine changed, sometimes on a daily basis, so it was very hard to hit the mark, leading to multiple overdoses. I was hospitalized seven times in less than a year. Bathing and eating fell further and further down the list of priorities until eventually they just seemed like a complete waste of time. As soon as I stopped cleaning my track marks, they got infected and abscesses formed on my arms. Eventually they were all over my body. Many times I would miss a vein and I would get cysts and those would become infected, too. Paranoia was a constant and quickly turned into a cocaine-induced psychosis. I began having violent rages and Jennifer and I fought constantly, which often got physical. We lived in hotels and carried knives to protect ourselves, and several times we nearly stabbed each other. Her family was trying to find us so they could put her in rehab, so we kept moving to stay ahead of them. And somehow all of this seemed normal.

Her family eventually got a message through to us. Jennifer's grandmother had died and left her a bunch of money. She had been an author and all the publishing income would now be going directly to Jennifer. I know what you're thinking: how fast did we spend it all on drugs? But we actually had a moment of clarity and decided this would be how we finally got clean. We got an apartment on the beach because I was certain if I could see the water, feel the sun, and get into the ocean every day, I'd stay clean. I wouldn't be depressed anymore.

We got all new furniture, really nice stuff we told each other was too expensive to ruin. We ignored the fact that this was the third time we'd moved into a new place with new furniture in an attempt to stay clean. We even made the same pact with each other we'd made at the previous two: "We're not going to do drugs in this apartment."

We lasted fewer than 48 hours before we were shooting up on our brand new furniture in our beautiful new apartment. We shut the blinds on our magnificent ocean view and never opened them again.

I didn't realize how bad I had gotten until a friend of mine named Christian came from Vancouver to visit. He took one look at me and said, "I'll give you $15,000 if you can stop using for a week."

I was high, so I wasn't sure I'd heard him right. "Fifteen grand?"

"In cash."

"That's fucking stupid," I said. "Are you kidding me?"

"No, I'm not kidding."

"That's the dumbest fucking...do you honestly think I'm going to lose this bet?"

"I don't want you to lose the bet. I want you to win," he replied.

It didn't make any sense to me. Why did he choose that dollar amount and what was his motivation? Either way, I was so excited to get that 15 grand. It was going to be the easiest 15 grand I'd ever made.

"You're on," I said.

We shook on it, and I started thinking about what I was going to do with all that cash. I lasted until that evening. It was getting dark out and I knew the dealers in Santa Monica would be closing down shop soon. I was humiliated. I couldn't look him in the eye when I said, "Can we start tomorrow?"

He was so disappointed in me. I saw it in his eyes. "Yes, of course we can start tomorrow."

Tomorrow never came. I couldn't go more than a few hours without shooting up or smoking crack.

✳ ✳ ✳

Things got progressively worse from there. Jennifer and I bounced in and out of The Telesis Foundation, an outpatient detox center run by another crazy old man named Jerry. If we went to the treatment meetings, he would give us medication to help with our withdrawal—Valium, Xanax, Vicodin, Soma. We would pay extra and get the buprenorphine because the results were guaranteed. Plus we loved shooting coke with it because it took the edge off.

The other great thing about Telesis was that you met some of the coolest people there. There's certainly no shortage of drug abuse in the entertainment industry. It was at Telesis that I learned to never say, "Wow, man, you look just like so-and-so," because 10 times out of 10 it *was* so-and-so and I wound up completely embarrassing myself.

I became friends with one of these people who, for anonymity purposes, we'll just call Steve. Much to our surprise, Steve was even cooler in person than he was on screen, which didn't seem possible. He had the greatest stories about everyone in the business and he got the most amazing coke from Hollywood. I was already buying top quality heroin by this time, at wholesale prices. It all seemed too good to be true.

I introduced him to Jennifer and the rest of the gang up at Manny's house, and everyone loved him instantly. We started partying together for days at a time. One night, toward the end of a bender, we found ourselves back at Manny's house. I was acutely paranoid from shooting too much coke and getting zero sleep for several days. As I wandered around the party, I spotted Jennifer and Steve having a very intense conversation.

I didn't think anything of it. Steve and I had bought several ounces of coke and heroin and I was holding the latter.

I was sharply focused on getting upstairs to shoot up. When I came back downstairs, they were sitting right next to each other, whispering and giggling.

I couldn't believe it. How could I have missed something so obvious? I was already jealous of Steve and his success, and now the motherfucker was trying to steal my girlfriend? The way Jennifer looked at him drove me to the edge.

I walked over to them. "Give me some of the coke."

"We don't have any more," Steve said. "Give us some of your heroin."

"Fuck you," I said. "Give me some of the coke."

"Seriously, it's all gone."

I didn't believe them. They were holding out on me, keeping it between the two of them like a secret. I stormed off and did the only logical thing I could think to do next—I smoked some crack. As if I weren't paranoid enough already, now I was fucking psychotic. I watched the two of them intently. They glanced at me, saw me staring, and started whispering again. I stormed over and started flipping out on Jennifer.

"Why would you lie to me?! I know you guys have more coke! Fuck both of you! I don't even care. Go do whatever you want. You're a fucking idiot!"

This type of scenario between the two of us was unfortunately very common. I would get high, I would scream at her, call her names, and threaten to kill myself if she ever left me. I would beg her to never abandon me, to never leave me alone, and she would tell me we'd always be together. It happened hundreds of times.

I went on and on, cursing, yelling, and putting her down. I thought for sure Steve was gonna say something to break up the scene I was causing, or even worse, interject to stand up for her. He was quite a bit bigger than I was and, from what I had heard, a pretty tough motherfucker. But I was possessed. And he knew it. The drugs and the rage peeled back the usual mask that I wore to please everyone and revealed the darkness within. Neither of them dared say a word. They simply endured my onslaught of visceral hatred, insults, and threats. I stomped upstairs like a petulant child and locked myself in one of the bathrooms so I could smoke the rest of the crack that I had stashed in my pocket. Sometime later—I don't know how long I was gone—I walked around the party looking for the two of them. They were gone.

I asked everyone, "Where are Jennifer and Steve?"

Nobody knew.

"You fucking idiots! Where are they?!"

It was getting close to one in the morning. The party was approaching the turning point where everyone was way too high, the drugs were gone, and tempers flared. The crowd began trickling out of Manny's house. I followed, convinced I was going to find Jennifer and Steve hooking up somewhere outside.

I did find them. They were walking away, leaving the party together. Leaving me behind. I died on the inside. I knew what that meant. They were going to score more drugs, get high, and have sex. I couldn't handle it.

Well, fuck her, I thought. *This is it. Now I'm really going to do it. I'm going to kill myself.*

I went inside, upstairs, and shot a little more heroin. When I came back downstairs, I saw that the last of the crowd was leaving and I was happy about that.

I thought, *Fuck them. I'm never going to see them again anyway, fucking assholes.*

Pretty soon Manny was the only one left, completely wasted and passed out on his bed. I went back upstairs into the kitchen and grabbed a giant spoon and a 27-gauge intramuscular needle. Then I took all the heroin I had left, close to a gram and a half, and cooked it all up. I drew every last drop into the syringe and triumphantly shot it all into my arm.

I immediately felt warm.

I started to float.

Then I was somewhere else. It was very cold and dark, but I was completely awake and aware. I didn't feel high at all. I was lucid and trying to figure out what was going on. Then it dawned on me.

Oh my God! Oh my God!

Oh fuck fuck fuck fuck.

I did it.

I'm dead.

Oh my God. Oh fuck.

My vision started to cloud in the cold darkness, then it shifted. I was looking down at myself lying on the floor of Manny's kitchen.

Oh my God. I'm dead.

Manny raced past my body in slow motion. He was on the phone. He ran to the freezer, came back, and knelt over me. He did something to my neck and ran back to the freezer. This happened several times, and I could see he was packing ice cream around my neck.

What the fuck? Ice cream?

Then I realized he was trying to preserve my brain—for when I woke up.

Good luck.

Fuck, I'm dead.

I'm really dead.

A group of strangers rushed into the room. They moved Manny away and crowded around me. I saw paramedic uniforms and firefighter gear. They cut my shirt off and checked my vitals. A terrible pain ripped through my chest.

BAM!

Fuck!

That's it.

It's almost over.

I'm going.

The first responders worked furiously over my body. The sharp pain hit me again.

BAM!

All of a sudden I wasn't above my body anymore. I was below it, looking up through the earth and floor. My chest jerked with the strange, consuming pain for the third time.

BAM!

I heard voices.

"No, nothing, nothing. We don't have anything."

"Do it again."

"Clear!"

There was a loud beeping and then again, BAM!

My eyes flew open.

"Wait, wait, wait. We got him. We got him."

A vivid rustling sound filled my ears.

"We're losing him. We're losing him. Go again."

BAM!

The pain was excruciating. I opened my eyes again. They had an oxygen mask over my face. The people around me were in a flurry of activity. They put me on a stretcher and carried me out to the ambulance. On the way I passed one of the guys from the party. He was horrified by what he saw.

I just fucking died.

I just fucking died.

They put me in the ambulance and we sped toward the hospital. A female paramedic held my hand and slapped it when I started to fade away again.

"Stay with us. Stay with us."

I looked over at her.

She said, "Think about the good times. Think about the happy times. Think good thoughts."

I tried to talk through the haze and the oxygen mask, but only managed to let out a weak moan.

"I can't understand you," she said.

I pointed at the mask.

She slid it off as she repeated, "Think happy thoughts. Think about the good times."

"There aren't any," I said.

She started to tear up. I was already crying. I shook my head.

"I'm sorry, there aren't any. I don't have any."

She put the oxygen mask back on and held my hand. They took me to St. John's Hospital in Santa Monica, where the doctors asked me a bunch of questions.

"What did you inject?"

"Heroin."

"How much?"

"A lot."

"Was that intentional? Did you intend to overdose?"

I was honest. "Yes, it was intentional."

I could tell the staff was not happy about me being there. They rushed through their tasks and ignored me whenever they could. I was incredibly thirsty and kept asking for water, but they wouldn't bring me any. I finally asked a nurse, "Hey, man, could you guys lighten up a little bit?"

He took a deep breath, trying to control his temper. "There are innocent people here who have been in accidents. There are people here fighting for their lives. Some of them aren't going to make it. And then there's you, just throwing your fucking life away for drugs."

I was taken off guard by his honesty. I had no defense. They'd shot me up with Narcan so I was completely sober, and I knew he was right. I wanted to crawl under the bed and hide. I wanted to get the hell out of the hospital. Most of all, pathetically, I wanted to get high again. I was starting to get dopesick. The doctor had given me some sedatives but they couldn't touch what I was about to go through. I was close to ripping the IVs out and making a break for it when the doctor came back in.

"Here's what's going to happen," he said. "We're doing a shift change in about 45 minutes. When that happens, the hospital is legally obligated to report this as a suicide attempt. You'll be 5150'd and you will go to jail."

A 5150 meant I could be involuntarily confined as a danger to myself or others. I'd been arrested and held overnight several times and the thought of going through heroin withdrawal in a cold cell made me start crying immediately. "I don't want to go to fucking jail! I don't want to be arrested!"

The doctor said, "You can check yourself out now, or you can wait around for the shift change. Up to you."

"I'll go now."

I think they just wanted to get rid of me, which was completely understandable. They started unplugging the IVs and

monitors. All I had were my jeans and a wad of cash. No
socks, shoes, or shirt—the paramedics had cut it off me to
use the defibrillator. Maybe Jennifer had thought to bring
something for me to wear besides the hospital gown. I asked
the doctor, "Where is everybody?"

"What are you talking about?"

"My friends. Can they come in now?"

"What friends?"

I was confused. Of course Manny had called Jennifer and
Steve and everyone else to let them know what had happened. They all had to be worried sick about me, anxious to
come in and make sure I was okay.

"My friends," I said. "Who's here with me?"

The doctor said, "There's nobody here for you."

I brushed it off. Knowing them, they were all high and
afraid to come in because they might get busted, so they had
to be waiting for me in the parking lot. I shuffled outside,
cramping and sweating from the withdrawal. I searched for
five minutes before I realized no one was there.

No friends, no Jennifer, no anyone. No one cared. It didn't
matter if I lived or died. So I took a taxi to Santa Monica and
armed myself to the teeth with drugs, then went and got a
hotel. I was going to finish the job.

But first I called everyone and left scathing messages. Jennifer, Steve, everyone.

"How dare you! Fuck you! I fucking hate you!"

Jennifer and her sister used the Caller ID to get the hotel's
address. Jennifer tried to talk to me but I threw her out of
the hotel room. She'd cheated on me with Steve and I didn't
want to see her. I see the ridiculous hypocrisy of this now, of
course, but at the time I only felt heartbreak. Then Manny

and Steve showed up.

I screamed at Steve, "How could you do that to me?!"

He was baffled. "Do what? What are you talking about?"

"You left with my girlfriend, man. You—"

"Dude, you disappeared upstairs and locked yourself in the fucking bathroom, so I gave her a ride home. That's all. Nothing happened."

They talk a lot about hitting bottom in 12-step programs. I had definitely hit bottom. But always true to form and never knowing anything other than extremes, when I hit bottom, I got a shovel out and started digging. And I would keep digging for the next four years.

* * *

Maybe it was my near-successful suicide attempt, or the fact that we were using Jennifer's dead grandmother's money to get high, but over the next few months something changed in her. She kept talking about getting clean, and in a rare moment of sobriety she decided to go to Europe. She begged me to go with her. I rattled off a list of bullshit reasons—my music, my friends, whatever—but I could have gone. I should have gone.

When she left there was $37,000 in the checking account. She came back three weeks later and only $11,000 remained. I'd managed to shoot well over $20,000 worth of drugs into my arm while she was away. I weighed 109 pounds. I had staph infection, ringworm, and scabies, which I picked up while scoring drugs on Skid Row.

Jennifer walked in, took one quick look around, and said, "Where's mine?"

I cooked her up a speedball and we were off to the races together again. When the money ran low we pawned the family heirlooms she'd inherited from her grandmother. The last thing we sold was a beautiful six carat diamond necklace. We got $7,000 for it and headed straight to downtown LA. We never even made it home with the drugs. We pulled over on the side of the road and shot up and shot up and shot up. I tore my face apart in the rearview mirror trying to get the bugs that I thought were crawling on me.

On the way home, we fought viciously. I kept yelling at her to switch seats with me and drive. I was psychotic—talking to myself and seeing things—but in a few brief moments of lucidity I realized I should not be driving a car. Jennifer refused to drive. Unlike me, instead of becoming crazed and animated when she was high, she became shut down, lethargic, and despondent. I drove fast, trying to prove a point, trying to scare her. I was doing about 75 miles an hour when I decided to shoot up some more coke to stay awake. This was not unusual—I had been shooting up and driving for quite some time. I had become somewhat of an expert at driving with my knees while managing a crack pipe or a syringe. I pushed off and very quickly realized I had done too much. My vision started to dart from side to side which, when you're shooting coke, is never a good sign.

The impact came quickly. A lot of times, when you're in an accident, things move in slow motion, but this was brief and sudden and violent. I took out five mailboxes before hitting a parked car, crashing through a fence, and rolling the vehicle several times before landing in someone's front yard. That someone, by some bizarre twist of fate, happened to be the secretary of the Tuesday night Narcotics Anonymous meeting in Malibu.

The car landed upright, the hood propped open and the engine compartment on fire. The man ran into his house, grabbed a fire extinguisher, and quickly put the flames out. He then came over to the driver's side door to see if I was okay and help me out of the car. But I wouldn't get out. I yelled at him to leave me alone.

"What are you doing?" he asked.

"I've gotta get my balloons. I spilled them everywhere."

How fucking high must I have been to say that? High or stupid; both, I suppose. This was the secretary of the Narcotics Anonymous meeting—he knew that by "balloons," I meant "packages of heroin and cocaine."

Within minutes, all the neighbors had come outside. It was 4:40 in the morning and I could hear the sirens. How do I remember it was 4:40 in the morning? Because the man had now gone back inside, grabbed a baseball bat, and was screaming at me, "You fucking piece of shit! If it were 20 minutes later, my wife would have been leaving for work and you could have killed her!"

Jennifer and I got out of the car and went and sat on the curb as the paramedics and police simultaneously arrived. The man immediately started yelling at the cop, "That fucking piece of shit is a heroin addict and he's on drugs right now. You need to arrest him!"

He kept repeating it as he lunged at me. One of the cops held him back and when he finally gave up, the cop asked, "How do you know that he's a heroin addict?"

And the man said, "Because I'm the fucking secretary of the NA meeting on Tuesday night and I know exactly who this piece of shit is. He's a junkie."

To which the cop replied (and to this day I still can't believe it), "I thought it was an anonymous program."

I was stunned. Jennifer was stunned. The man was *certainly* stunned. The same cop came over and asked me point-blank, "Are you intoxicated right now?"

"Yes, officer," I said with no hesitation.

"On what?" he asked.

"Drugs. Heroin, cocaine...I can't remember what else, maybe some pills."

The cop seemed somewhat perplexed by my transparency. "Do you have any drugs on you right now?"

And again with no hesitation I said, "Yes. I've got heroin and coke on me and some needles."

Now he wasn't just perplexed; he was astounded that I would volunteer all of this information.

"Hang on for a second," he said.

He walked back over and asked the man if anyone else had been hurt in the accident. The man pointed back at the two of us and said, "No, just them."

Then the cop went over and talked to a few of the other officers. They spoke in hushed tones. After a few minutes, the same cop came back over and spoke to me.

"Are either of you badly injured?"

"No, I'm just a little bit scraped up," I said. I was lying.

He said, "Okay. When the paramedics come over, you can simply refuse medical attention and I'll call you a cab."

I thought for a second I was dreaming. This guy wasn't actually going to let me go, was he?

"Wait, I can leave?"

"Yes," he responded. "You can refuse medical attention and a cab should be arriving shortly. I would suggest you get in it and you get out of here as fast as you can."

Then he put his hand on my shoulder, looked me dead in the eyes, and said, "This is it. This is your moment of clarity. Go tomorrow and get some fucking help. I'm letting you go for various reasons, which you don't deserve, but take this opportunity and get your shit together."

We got home and barricaded ourselves inside the apartment. The water had been shut off and we thought people were coming for us. Turns out they were. Days later I woke up to Jennifer's father standing over me saying, "You're going to die if you don't get help."

He dragged us out through the door he'd broken down and took us to a treatment center down in Orange County called Spencer Recovery Center. The last thing I saw in that apartment was my own blood smeared on the bathroom wall:

GOD HELP ME

CHAPTER FIVE

I WAS FINALLY IN REHAB. AND I HADN'T BROKEN IN JUST TO get meds like the last time; I was checked in with a wristband, a room, all of it. When the medical staff heard how much dope I'd been shooting, they looked gravely concerned. Five grams of heroin along with five to seven grams of cocaine was a typical day. They loaded me up on a range of narcotics to battle the withdrawal symptoms. I actually felt optimistic about everything at first. I knew this was the best—and probably only—chance Jennifer and I had to finally get clean.

They drugged the shit out of us, took away our cell phones, and let us loose to meet all of the other clients who were outside smoking. Heroin addicts gravitate toward other heroin addicts. You could be in a room of a thousand people and if there was one other junkie there, within a few minutes of arriving you would lock eyes, just like vampires, and immediately have a quiet, unspoken understanding. It takes a certain kind of person to go that far down the rabbit hole. You must possess an immense amount of pain, intelligence, bravery, stupidity, and hubris.

So not surprisingly, we quickly found the other heroin addicts and started to bond and share drug-a-logues. We smoked cigarettes like fucking beatniks, lighting one off of the other, our pulses racing with adrenaline and excitement in the strange process of show and tell. We compared track marks, abscesses, scars, and bruises. I quickly learned the lay of the land and found out that quite a few patients had left and gotten high and were allowed to come back.

Fuck it, I thought. *If those people were allowed back in, I'll get in, too.*

One of the other junkies was a super thin, creepy guy named Peter who was always smoking and complaining about everything. He sounded like I felt and I figured he wanted the same thing I did. I got him alone and said, "I wanna get fucking high, man. I wanna get high."

He didn't hesitate. "Let's go. Let's go tonight."

I wasn't ready for that response. "Tonight? How?"

"I have my car here."

"You have your car at rehab?"

"Yeah. I'm staying across the street in the Bellagio." The Bellagio was what we called the fancier area of Spencer Recovery Center because it was on the beach and had much nicer rooms; it also cost double. I was staying in the part we called the Dog House because it had a long and narrow paved alleyway alongside it where everybody smoked and we called that the Dog Run.

"I can leave any time I want," he said. "We'll go get high and then come back. It's no big deal."

That didn't really sound like rehab to me. "Are you sure?"

"Just meet me out front tonight."

Easy for him to say. He was in the Bellagio and could

come and go as he pleased. I was on the second floor of the main building, which was locked down at night. Lights-out came and everyone went to their rooms. I made sure no one was outside in the hallway and managed to pry my window open. The building next door had a roof that was about level with the bottom of my window and slanted away down to one story. The Dog Run was below me and I'd have to jump the width of it to land on the roof. I couldn't judge the exact distance in the dark. It was obviously a stupid and dangerous plan, but there was heroin on the other end of that jump. So I jumped.

I didn't make it. I barely caught the edge of the roof with my hands. I knew if I dropped I'd break a leg, an arm, maybe my neck. Adrenaline shot through me and I pulled myself up to safety. I rolled down the slanted roof and fell onto the ground, about an eight-foot drop. I didn't feel any pain as I ran toward the waiting car, only excitement. I was exhilarated. I felt like I had just broken out of prison and I knew within a short time, I'd be high as a fucking kite.

We drove for an hour and a half to North Hollywood because Peter owned a factory there that made costume jewelry.

I must have asked him about 20 times on the way, "You have fresh rigs, right?"

"Yeah, of course."

"And clean points?" I wanted to make absolutely sure he had new syringes and needles.

"Yes," he said. He called his dealer on the way and told him to meet us at the factory. We got there around one o'clock in the morning and bought $1,200 worth of heroin and coke. I almost didn't make it to the toilet. Something strange happens the moment you know you're gonna score dope—your bowels immediately want to evacuate. If you're a drug addict, you know what I'm talking about. I was dry heaving as well, another strange reaction my body would have once I knew I had drugs and was about to shoot them into my arm. I came out of the bathroom with the hunger and craving of a hundred men.

"Where are the needles?" I barked at Peter.

He pointed to a desk. I quickly walked over and started pulling open all the drawers. Almost every one was filled with needles, all of them bent, bloody, and rusty with clotted syringes.

"Are you fucking kidding me?! I asked you 10 times if you had clean rigs!"

He was too busy cooking up a speedball to respond.

I grabbed the least damaged syringes and started rinsing them in hot water. We spent the rest of the night shooting up every last bit of our score. I heard voices and saw figures in the shadows as I sat slumped over in a puddle of my own blood. Peter kept handing me bloody syringes that he had just shot up with. After a while I didn't even bother to rinse them with water. What difference would it make? At one point I asked him, "Are you clean? I mean, do you have anything?"

He shot me a demonic look, "Do *you*?!"

"No," I said, not really knowing for sure whether I did or didn't. This certainly wasn't the first time I'd shared needles. By the time the sun came up, all rational thought had been completely replaced by paranoia and psychosis. We argued through the whole trip back to rehab about whose fault it was that we were going to get caught.

I felt so disgusting and dirty. My mouth tasted like metal and sin. I had a horrible tooth infection and an abscess inside my mouth the size of a grape. The sun burned my eyes as we drove. The cigarettes seemed to be burning my lungs to a crisp. My fingernails had black gunk underneath them—a combination of blood, filth, and heroin. I had bloodstains on my pants and shirt. I dared not look in the mirror.

When we pulled into Spencer Recovery Center, one of the staff members grabbed Peter and took him straight back to the Bellagio. I was taken to the main office and reprimanded. They were taking turns playing good cop/bad cop. But in the end, they let me stay.

I staggered out of the office in tears, swearing that I was never going to get high again. In the hallway the nurse who issued our medications grabbed me and pulled me aside. She and I got along really well and she always tried to make my stay more comfortable.

"You didn't shoot up with Peter, did you?" she asked.

Her intensity made me pause. "Why?"

"Did you share needles with him?"

I lied. "No, why?"

She said, "Because he has AIDS and Hepatitis C."

"How in the fuck do you know that?"

She looked at me like I was an idiot. "Because I'm the *nurse*, Khalil. I give everyone their meds."

"Oh, right."

"Khalil, did you share needles with him?"

"No," I firmly repeated.

I was trying to convince myself more than her. I didn't want to believe that I had shared needles with someone who had full-blown AIDS. But I had. I couldn't take it. It ate away at me. I couldn't sleep and a couple days later the doctor cut me off from all my meds. Their policy was to medicate for the first nine days of your stay, then allow you a full three weeks to completely get over the withdrawal.

"I'm sick," I said.

"You're just going to have to go through it."

I yelled "fuck you" and walked out—out of his office and out of rehab. I couldn't handle getting dopesick *and* the stress of having shared needles with Peter. I found Jennifer and told her I was leaving, but that I'd come back for her. We were going to be together forever and both of us knew it. On my way out of the building I ran into another patient, a super wealthy dentist from somewhere in Washington, who said he wanted to leave too but wasn't ready to pull the trigger yet.

He gave me the keys to his car, which was parked two streets over, and handed me his wallet. All his cards had the same PIN and he gave that to me, too. He was desperate to get some dope. He told me to go get cash, buy the drugs, and bring them back to him. He wanted to get high one more time before he decided to stay or go.

"Will you do that for me?" he asked. "Will you bring me the stuff here tonight?"

"Yeah, sure," I said. "I'll be back tonight. You've got nothing to worry about, man. I'm gonna go get a bunch of shit and bring it back. I can climb up onto the building next door and throw it right through your window. I'll see you tonight at 1:00 a.m."

I was gone for four days. I did what any good drug addict would do: I got a hotel room, a bunch of needles, crack, heroin, and coke, and began indoor surfing. I filled the syringe to capacity and pushed off into sweet oblivion.

On the fourth day I had a moment of clarity and realized the dentist was still waiting for me. He'd been calling my cell phone non-stop since I'd left rehab. I picked up the phone and called Spencer Recovery Center, but not for the dentist. I wanted to let Jennifer know I was still alive. The receptionist answered and I asked for Jennifer.

"Oh, she's not here."

"What do you mean, she's not there?"

"She left."

"That's impossible. She didn't fucking leave. Just please get Jennifer."

"She's not here," she repeated.

I said, "Look, I know they told you to say that, because it's me, but just please go get her. I really need to talk to her."

"No, man, seriously. Hold on."

She left the phone and I tried to make sense of what she'd said. Jennifer wouldn't leave. She'd never leave me. Never.

A female patient who Jennifer and I both knew picked up on the other end. "Hey, Khalil. Yeah, Jennifer left. Her mom came with some dudes and they took her."

Jennifer's family had hired a specialist named Warren Boyd, a.k.a. "The Cleaner." He and his team had drugged her, snatched her up, and sequestered her under constant guard to keep her from running back to me. I threw the phone across the room and shot up even more. I started having seizures from all the coke. Once I came to I shot up with heroin and passed out. I was trying to kill myself again but I kept waking up.

I don't know how many rounds of this I survived. I only stopped because somebody started pounding on the door. It was the hotel manager.

"You've been in here for three days," she yelled. "You're not supposed to be here anymore. We need the room back."

I had a cloudy memory of one of the maids coming in while I was nodding off. They didn't need the room back—they just wanted me out. I went back to Santa Monica, loaded up on more drugs, then drove straight back to Spencer Recovery Center, steering with my knees most of the way so I could shoot up, to see what the fuck was going on with Jennifer.

When I pulled in the dentist was waiting out front for me. He was furious but he only had one question for me: "Do you have anything?"

"I've got everything."

"Do you know how to shoot someone up?" he asked.

"Of course I do." I cooked up a speedball and shot it into his arm, which immediately erased his bad mood. He wanted to go get more and in my excitement I forgot about Jennifer. We went back to Marina del Rey and got a hotel room near LAX and went to work. We bought thousands of dollars' worth of heroin, crack, and cocaine and got high for 10 days straight.

Toward the end of the 10 days he started saying he needed to stop, that he couldn't take it anymore. He kept calling his wife back in Washington, crying, telling her he missed her and wanted to come home. One time while he was talking to her, he shoved a bunch of cash at me, covered the mouthpiece, and told me to go get more drugs. I figured he was embarrassed about the phone call. I wanted to give him some privacy so I hurried out. When I got back with the drugs, he was gone. He'd packed all his things and left.

I couldn't believe it. I was crushed. When you do drugs

with someone—especially coke—you make all these big promises and vows to one another. He and I had made huge plans, including both of us getting into another rehab facility and getting clean at some point. But when you sober up, all that shit goes out the window. You don't care about anyone. I was alone again. Except for the money and the drugs he'd left with me.

The hotel was near Century and Sepulveda on the border of Inglewood, and at three o'clock in the morning I walked out underneath the overpass where the homeless crackheads hung out. I was so high that I waved hundred dollar bills in front of them and screamed at them to go get me more crack.

I shoved the cash at a few of them. They took it and immediately ran away and of course none of them came back with my crack. I wish all of them had done that, but a few started following me instead of running away. I walked back to the hotel room to get more money and, because my key had stopped working, I had the security lock stuck between the door and the jamb so it wouldn't close all the way. I grabbed the cash and hit the street again, only this time I actually got drugs; some homeless dude took me to a dealer and I scored a bunch of heroin and crack.

I raced back to the hotel. As soon as I got in the room I knew something was wrong. I saw shadows moving along the wall and caught a glimpse of someone's dirty flannel shirt peeking over the top of the second bed, between the bed and the wall. I ran into the bathroom as not one but two guys jumped up and lunged at me. I made it into the bathroom and locked the door. I grabbed the porcelain lid off of the toilet tank and stood up on the counter in the darkness, ready to swing. Every inch of me was trembling.

After shooting up and not sleeping for days, this wasn't the most convenient time to have to fight for my life.

The first bullet punched a hole in the door. The shot was deafening and a beam of light poured into the bathroom. Then they fired again. I screamed and slammed the lid against the door.

"I'll fucking kill you! I'll fucking kill you!"

I slammed the lid against the door over and over until it broke in half, slicing my hand badly. I dove from the counter into the bathtub and for whatever reason turned the water on, as if that was going to protect me or something. I lay there in that tub with the cold water coming down on me, shaking, bleeding, and crying, waiting for them to come in and kill me. I thought about my life—how the whole thing was one big mistake, how badly I had behaved, all the people I had mistreated, how much it sucked that this is how it was going to end, in a bathtub at a cheap hotel in Inglewood. I clenched my eyes shut as I anticipated the gunshot to the forehead or heart and prayed that it would be sudden, quick, and painless.

They never came. I turned off the water. It sounded like they were gone, but I lay there for another 20 minutes just to be safe. Finally I stood up and inspected the bullet holes in the door. They were small, probably fired from a .22 or .25 caliber. Someone had shot at me and had tried to kill me. I was suddenly hit with a wave of nausea. I began throwing up, mostly dry heaving because nothing was inside of me. Then I passed out right there on the bathroom floor.

When I woke up hours later, I was lying in the bed. The kind, thin, vaguely familiar face of a black man came into focus. He had grey stubble and short salt and pepper hair. He held a compress to my forehead. I tried to jump up but he held me down. I was weak and dehydrated. He kept making me drink water. I didn't understand where he'd come from. To this day it still baffles me. I felt like I knew him and he acted like he knew me, but what the fuck was he doing in that hotel? How did he find me?

I passed out again. When I came to this time, the man was gone. The compress laid on the night stand. It wasn't a dream. Was he an angel?

* * *

I threw what little I still had from rehab—some clothes, headphones, a toothbrush—into my backpack and ran out of the hotel. I was sure that somebody was waiting to kill me around every corner. I walked carefully, scanning my periphery, to another cheap hotel in Inglewood where a couple of prostitutes were hanging out front.

"Can you guys get me some heroin?" I asked them. They looked at me and laughed like I was stupid.

"How much?" one of them said.

They could only get me coke. Who was I to argue?

Obviously I had learned nothing from my most recent brush with death because when I went to pay her, I pulled out a big wad of cash and peeled off a hundred dollar bill. She brought me the coke and I went back to my room and started shooting up. It was all I had left—the heroin and the crack were long gone. I heard a bunch of voices in the hallway outside my room and immediately pulled the mattress off the bed frame and shoved it in front of the door, followed by the dresser.

They must have heard me. They started pounding on the door. I heard muffled voices and laughter. When you're high on coke, you gain an acute hearing ability and I could make out the voice of a woman: "No, he's got money. He's got a bunch of money. I saw it, I saw it!"

I sat there in the dark, shooting up again and again. I had multiple seizures. My whole left arm went cold and numb and I felt an incredible pain and pressure on my chest. And then I saw it: the shadowy, demonic figure from my nightmares as a child, except this time there wasn't just one. The room was full of them. They were racing around the walls, clawing and attacking me. The darkness those creatures embodied wanted nothing less than my soul for all eternity. I raced to the bathroom and pulled the shower curtain bar down and started swinging at them. Meanwhile, the pounding on the door got louder and more violent.

At some point in the midst of all this, I passed out.

I woke up the next afternoon on the bathroom floor. Someone was knocking on the door.

I staggered over to it and stood to the side in case they fired. "Who is it?"

"The manager. You were supposed to check out two hours ago."

"Oh, sorry. I'm just getting my stuff together. I'll be down in five minutes." I was filthy. I got in the shower and when the water hit my back, the pain was incredible. I couldn't figure out why it hurt so badly—this wasn't withdrawal, something was wrong. Had I gotten more cuts from the porcelain toilet lid at the last hotel? But how would they be on my back?

I stood on a towel in front of the mirror and turned

around to get a better look. My back was covered in claw marks. I flashed back to the previous night. Something had come for me in that hotel room and had gouged my flesh too many times to count. I don't know if they were demons, ghosts, or something else entirely, but they had come for me and had tried to tear me apart.

The tiny remaining rational part of my mind said, *Yeah, that's fucking impossible. This isn't some horror film. It didn't happen. You must have rubbed against something on the mattress.*

Every other part of me knew it was true. It was as real as anything I've ever experienced in my life. This wasn't just spiritual warfare anymore. Now, through my reckless actions and total disregard for my life, I had unequivocally invited evil in.

I quickly dismissed these thoughts. I had no time to debate with myself. I called a taxi and drove to the pawn shop where Jennifer and I had pawned her grandmother's necklace, which was actually close by. When you pawn something, especially expensive jewelry, you have to give them your driver's license and fingerprints. We had used mine because Jennifer was scared of getting in trouble with her family.

Since it was under my name, I told them I was no longer interested in getting the necklace back and I wanted to get the other half of the money instead. Once again, I was loaded with cash. I made my way back to downtown LA. By this point, I was severely dopesick. I shot the rest of my coke in the back of the taxi to try to stave off the heroin withdrawal, which is a horribly dangerous game to play.

I eventually scored some tar and "got well." As usual, I did too much and needed to lie down. I stumbled to a nearby alley and made my way to the ground. It smelled like hot garbage and stale vomit. There was a giant pile of human feces within arm's length from me. Then it hit me. It hit me like a shovel to the head. It was all over. There was no coming back from where I was.

I had shared needles with somebody who had AIDS. I had no one to turn to and nobody could help me. My mother was living below the poverty level and I'd already drained whatever extra resources she had. She had borrowed thousands and thousands of dollars on her credit card to send me money.

The next 14 to 18 months—I don't really know the exact time frame—are a hazy blur of panhandling at gas stations, getting beat up, overdosing, and winding up in the hospital. I had been "homeless" before—sleeping in hotels or in cars or couch surfing at friends' houses. But from the moment I was *really* homeless, I couldn't drop my standards fast enough. Picking up half smoked cigarettes out of ashtrays and smoking them or shitting in alleys with no toilet paper became the norm.

I was always on the move. You can't stop when it gets to that point. I don't mean the drugs; that's a given. I mean moving. You always have to be moving. There is a constant feeling of impending doom and proof of its existence around every corner: dealers you owe money to, gangs whose territory you are dealing in unknowingly who will kill you without blinking, street people—professional hustlers, crackheads, and junkies infected with AIDS who have lost all hope and will end your life for a $5 hit. The streets are filthy and smell like shit and piss. They're littered with broken crack pipes, dirty needles, blood, and sin. Drop-in centers and homeless shelters look sad during the day, but you could never imagine the transformation that takes place on Skid Row when nighttime and darkness take hold. The beatings, the murders—people die down there all the time, but you'll never hear about it because nobody cares about those people, otherwise they wouldn't be down there in the first place.

It's a vast collection of prisoners from the war we lost on drugs, mentally ill people (many of whom are veterans) who belong in hospitals but can't afford it, kids from broken homes, and/or victims of violence and sexual abuse. A swirling hustle and bustle of madness and addiction, loss of hope, sex trade, murder, violence, crime, and sin, all controlled and quarantined to an area of the city fewer than a few blocks from the police department, where nobody will notice and nobody will care.

Men, straight men, will rape another man in front of a group of other men who are laughing, just to show dominance or power. The violence is different from the fake and desensitizing violence we see on TV and in the movies. It is swift and sudden and leaves you gasping. Blood is much darker and much more abundant. And the sounds, the visceral and guttural sounds of real violence, will not only take the air from your lungs, but leave you numb for hours afterward, like your whole body was shot up with Novocain.

You can't believe what you've witnessed, so your mind pushes it down somewhere within you, into the subconscious, trying to protect you. Unfortunately, it almost always resurfaces, usually in the form of a panic attack or nightmare.

Every now and then I managed to track down an old friend or acquaintance from Malibu who had pity on me.

They drove downtown, gave me money and, of course, wanted me to score for them, so I would.

After seeing the condition I was in, they would get me a hotel room and tell me to shower up and get my life together, but please don't call them again. I assume they had expected to see the old Khalil instead of the 109-pound, emaciated, filthy version covered with sores and abscesses. It scared the shit out of them until, one by one, they were all gone.

CHAPTER SIX

THE LAST PERSON WHO TRIED TO HELP ME WAS MY OLD neighbor Dana who lived next door to Jennifer and me before we got shipped off to rehab. She invited me to take the bus out to Malibu so I could shower up and put some clean clothes on. When she opened the door and saw me, she started crying.

"How could you let this happen to yourself?" she said.

"I don't know. I don't know." I was crying, she was crying. I urged her to call her dealer and get some heroin sent to the apartment, which she did. We got high for three days straight. When everything was gone, she loaned me her car to go get more. I disappeared for four or five days, of course, and when I finally went back she flipped out on me.

"What the fuck is wrong with you? Why would you do that to me? I fucking trusted you!"

She had called the police and said I'd stolen her car. I demanded money so I could get out of Malibu and she refused. We screamed and yelled and eventually she gave in.

"Fine, I'll get you some fucking money," she said.

"Wait here."

She went into her bedroom. I went into the kitchen, where I knew she had her quarter jar for laundry. She must have had close to $200 in quarters and I drained it all into my bag. It was rare for me to steal—I was so much better at simply asking people for things. But I knew that given the condition I was in I would never be getting invited back, anyway.

Dana came back with the cash and we started arguing again. She threw the money at me. I grabbed it and took off.

I jumped on a bus back to downtown LA, which was at least a two-hour ride. By that point I hadn't gotten high in a few hours and I was starting to get dopesick again. As I held myself, rocking back and forth with both arms wrapped around my abdomen, I began to shiver. It was evening and the bus was filled mostly with housekeepers on their way home from work. I still remember their kind and gentle faces looking at me with empathy.

I got off the bus on La Brea. I'd been to some good crack houses there before. I beelined for the closest one and by the time I came out, I wasn't just high...I was *fucking* high. My heart felt like it was gonna explode. I clenched my teeth so hard, I was certain they were all going to crack like porcelain. I saw flashing lights everywhere I looked. I heard helicopters and voices. My ears were filled with what I can only describe as that ringing sound you hear when you walk into a 7-11. I felt the worms crawling on my arms, on my scalp, in my ears and eyes and mouth, making their way to my brain. They were coming—the aliens, the demons. They were coming to get me.

I crouched down behind a hedge of bushes. I shoved so

much crack into the pipe, it almost wouldn't light. And then BAM! A giant fogger. My mouth, throat, and lungs all went numb, then it was my entire face. I heard loud screeching noises like a train coming to a halt.

They're coming. I know they're coming. They're going to kill me.

I stood up to run but my legs were wobbly and my vision started darting back and forth. I fell down hard, smacking my hands on the pavement. They were coming. They were going to kill me. I rose to my feet and with all my strength and concentration, I broke into a sprint. As I came around the corner of Washington and La Brea, I saw two cop cars sitting in the parking lot of the Chevron gas station. The car doors were open on one of them and a policeman was sitting in the front seat, talking into his radio.

I had a hunch that these cops were part of the "they" who had come to kill me. But they didn't know that I was behind them. I somehow convinced myself that if I got into their car first, they wouldn't be able to shoot me. I ran as fast as I could and dove into the back of one of the patrol cars. The seats were hard and plastic and with a loud thud, I crashed into them face first.

"Don't shoot me! Don't shoot me! Don't shoot me!" I yelled. To say that I had startled them would be an understatement.

"WHAT THE FUCK ARE YOU DOING?!" one of the cops yelled.

"Please don't shoot me! Please don't shoot me!"

"What the fuck are you talking about?!" he shouted.

"Please don't shoot me!"

"Get out of the car and put your hands on your head!"

Hearing those words struck me instantly sober. The harsh

realization that I had just hurled myself into the back of a police car high on drugs, with a crack pipe in my back pocket, washed over me like an ice cold wave. I slowly and carefully maneuvered my way out of the car as I grabbed the crack pipe out of my pocket.

"What are you doing?" the cop asked.

If I shattered the pipe, they couldn't use it as evidence against me. I threw the pipe straight down onto the hot asphalt. It bounced twice and landed between us, perfectly intact.

He stared at it, then looked up at me and shook his head. "You are one dumb motherfucker. Why didn't you just throw it into the street?"

"Can I throw it now?" I asked.

"No. Put your hands above your head. You're under arrest." He pushed me up against the car and frisked me, then read me my rights and put me back in the patrol car. Looking down at my license he asked, "What kind of a name is Khalil?"

"It's Arabic. My father is Palestinian."

"My dad is Arabic, too," he said. "We don't need any help making our people look bad, and yet here you are acting like a fucking idiot. You should be ashamed of yourself."

"Can you please just let me go? I promise I'll get help."

He actually considered it for a moment but decided to run my name first. Dispatch came back with bench warrants for my arrest. Lots of them. Apparently I'd been absent for court dates, but I had no idea when they were or what they were for.

That night I began the long and arduous process of entering the Los Angeles County Jail. I cried the whole time. I had been locked up in the Texas jail on the weed bust and I'd been held in the Lost Hills Sheriff Station in Malibu, but this was different. I had heard stories about LA County Jail, but no matter how bad those stories were, there was nothing in the world that could have prepared me for what came next.

* * *

They moved me from room to room for processing. It was freezing and I felt the start of withdrawal creeping in. They stripped me down, did a cavity search, fingerprinted me, and took my mugshot. Then they put me in a place called the Glass House, across the street from LA County Jail, to wait to be transferred. The smell in there was disgusting, like decaying flesh. It was crowded with homeless people, gang bangers, murderers, rapists. There was no separation. I was in there for two days. By now, my withdrawal was in full force. I was unbearably nauseous. I broke out in a cold sweat and shivered uncontrollably. I tried to sleep, but no such luck.

When they did finally move me across the street to County Jail, it felt like some bizarre déjà vu. They stripped us down again and gave us uniforms to wear. I was so cold. I couldn't stop shaking and sweating at the same time. They moved us from room to room, yelling at us the entire time. The smells emanating from the inmates blended together to form the most disgusting, putrid stench I had ever experienced, even worse than the Glass House—shit, piss, blood, and cum mixed with sin and failure.

Each time they moved us into a new room, we had to sit on the ice-cold cement floor, crammed uncomfortably close together, my knees always in someone's back and someone's knees always in my back. I now knew what it felt like to be cattle.

When we got to the second room, I took my position on the floor, keeping my knees drawn tightly into my chest and my arms tucked inside of my shirt with my hands under my armpits to try to stay warm. I noticed one of the other inmates staring at me. He seemed a little out of place—this very handsome white guy with these big, icy-blue eyes—but when he spoke, everything changed. His teeth, or what was left of them rather, were appalling, black and rotten.

"First time?" he said.

"What?" I asked, confused at his question.

His raspy voice repeated, "Is this your first time, man?"

"First time what?"

He tilted his head and raised his voice. "Is this your first fucking time being processed?"

"Yes, no, I mean…I don't know, sort of…here…yeah. I mean, I've never been to LA County Jail before."

He ignored my babbling answer and cracked a giant, rotting, satanic smile as he said, "Welcome to the system, man."

"What do you mean?"

He laughed for what seemed like an eternity, until finally he said, "Welcome to the system, man. Once you come in, you never stop coming in."

"No, no, no," I said. "I was just too high. I jumped in the back of a cop car. No, I'm not doing this again. I'm not coming back."

He started cackling away again and this time a few other inmates joined in. I shuddered. His disgusting raspy voice kept ringing in my head: "Welcome to the system, man."

Waves of nausea kept hitting me as the horrible smell intensified. I began dry heaving. It smelled like pus, like death, like AIDS. I was rotting. We were rotting. We were all rotting.

One big colony of lepers, sinners, failures, outcasts, murderers, and thieves.

There were a few high-ranking gang members in there with me. Because of their status, they got to sleep on the few available benches. They took all the rolls of toilet paper and used them as pillows. The lower-ranking gang members made sure they weren't bothered by any of the other inmates. I was forced to use my hands to wipe my ass. It was all too much. I began vomiting and shitting at the same time.

There I was on the cell floor, writhing and crying, shaking and convulsing. Nobody cared. The other inmates laughed and stepped on me as they walked past to use the toilet.

"How's that dope treating you now, peckerwood?"

When I couldn't stand the mess anymore, I made the stupid mistake of waking up one of the senior gang members and asking him for the toilet paper he was using as a pillow. He jumped up and one of the younger gang members clotheslined me, pulled me away, and yelled, "What the fuck you doin' boy? What the fuck you doin'? Don't look at him! What the fuck you doin'? Don't look at me!"

I looked away. He shoved me against the wall. When the gang leader settled back down onto the bench with his toilet paper pillow, the kid holding me lowered his voice. "Buddy, they're gonna fuck you up. You don't do that. You don't ever do that. You gotta get out of here."

I was confused at the sudden shift in his aggression. "Yeah, of course I have to get out of here. What am I supposed to do?"

"Quiet down. Listen to me. You need to tell one of the guards you're gonna kill yourself."

"Why?"

"Just do it. You gotta get out of General Pop. They're gonna fuck you up. You gotta get out of General Population."

I was shaking worse than ever. "Okay. Okay. Thank you... What's your name?"

"Christopher Reefer."

I'm sure you can guess why I remember that name. I did exactly what Christopher said. I told one of the guards I was going to kill myself. I was convulsing and covered in vomit, shit, and piss, and he believed me. A bunch of guards came into the cell and grabbed me, threw me on the ground, and put me in four-point restraints. They dragged me up to what was called the Pill Pod.

It didn't seem so bad at first. There was a common area like in the Glass House, but it was much less crowded and had enough places for everyone to sit and lie down to sleep. Along the walls were locked cells with solid steel doors and small Plexiglas windows. They were for the inmates who couldn't be controlled or were actively trying to hurt themselves and others, not just talking about it like I was.

During my time at the Pill Pod, I met a black guy named Dragon and a white guy named Bird who had the word "PECKERWOOD" tattooed across his shoulders. He explained to me that was what they called white people in prison. Dragon and Bird gave me a crash course on life on the inside: markings and tattoos, hierarchy and gangs, etiquette and colloquialisms. They had both spent a good portion of their lives in and out of jail and gangs.

They explained to me that the unit we were in was called Psychiatric and very different from General Population. In General Population, neither of them would be able to associate with one another. They wanted to know how I wound up in the Pill Pod, so I told them about the toilet paper incident.

"He was sleeping on the bench?" Dragon asked.

"Yeah," I said. "Why?"

"And you woke him up?"

"Yeah. Why?" I repeated.

"Fuck man. You so lucky they didn't kill you right then and there. They choke you out with a wet towel and kill you just like that."

I told them about Christopher Reefer.

Dragon shook his head and said, "That dude saved your life."

Bird chimed in, "Fuckin' A, right man. You owe that dude."

So thank you Christopher Reefer, if you're out there.

As the evening wore on and meds were dispersed, an eerie calm set in—the quiet before the storm, I suppose. I managed to doze off a little, until I was startled awake by a loud pounding noise. I looked around until I saw a man inside one of the cells bashing his head against the Plexiglas window in the door. Blood was splattered everywhere. Another man started screaming and bashing *his* head against his door as well. And in a third cell, a man was smearing something that covered his entire window. I didn't understand what was happening.

I looked over and saw that Dragon was awake.

"What's going on?" I asked.

"Oh man. They do that all night. They bash their heads open and then write with the blood. They smear it all over the place. That other dude, that's shit. He's smearing his shit all over the windows like he's painting with it or something."

"Why the hell would they do that?"

"What the fuck you mean *why*?" he said. "This the Pill Pod, motherfucker. This the nut house. You in with the crazies now because you said you were gonna kill yourself."

So I had managed to find my way into the mental ward of the Los Angeles County Jail. This was a whole new kind of hell. Days seemed to last for weeks and I could feel my sanity beginning to slip away. The inmates screamed and bashed their heads and pounded on those doors all night while I lay awake sleepless, still going through withdrawal. Acute withdrawal takes about three to five days, but it takes weeks, sometimes months, before any type of decent sleep can be had. The food was fucking disgusting—a whole separate form of punishment. I slowly but surely resigned to the fact that this was going to be my life for a long, long time. I knew I was on probation. I even vaguely remembered violating that probation a couple of times already, so this was it. I was fucked. I tried collect-calling everyone whose number I could remember, but nobody would answer.

People ask me all the time about the overdoses or the seizures and if that scared me, but none of that shit really scared me (except for the one time I flatlined and actually died), but this shit scared me. I enjoyed the conversation my new roommates provided to kill the time, but I could feel in my gut that neither of them could be trusted and both were quite possibly dangerous, very dangerous.

The only upside was that the guards gave me some Robaxin for the muscle pain and spasms. Some of the other inmates were on Wellbutrin, and they would crush it up and snort it. I tried that and it seemed to really help, too, but who knows—maybe I was just happy to be snorting something.

When my court date finally came two and a half weeks later, they shackled my wrists and ankles to another inmate and put us on a bus with a bunch of other guys. The bus stopped at all the courthouses to let inmates on and off, and I was one of the last stops. It smelled like no one on the bus had seen a bar of soap or a toothbrush for months.

They dropped me off at the Malibu Courthouse and put me next to the public defender appointed to represent me.

"What are we going to do?" I asked.

He didn't look up from his paperwork. "What are *we* going to do? *I'm* going to go home after this. *You're* going to jail."

"What're you talking about?"

"You're on probation," he said. "You signed a piece of paper saying you wouldn't violate that probation and that if you did, you would be going to prison for 18 months. Well, guess what? Smoking crack and being in possession of paraphernalia is in violation of that. So you're going to jail. Well, actually, you're going to state prison."

Fuck.

In a last ditch effort, I called my mom from the payphone. I begged and pleaded for her to hire me a lawyer, and when that didn't work, I screamed and threatened.

"I'm sorry," she said. "Don't call me anymore. There's nothing I can do." They took me into the courthouse to see the judge. It was Judge Adamson, a woman I'd been in front of on several other occasions. She had always been very kind and understanding with me, and I was ashamed to have her see me in the condition I was in. I hung my head and waited for her to send me to prison.

She said, "We're going to bring up the person who is going to speak on your behalf."

I looked up from the floor. "What?"

"You have someone here to speak on your behalf."

I turned around. A woman I barely knew named Penny walked toward the bench. One of my panicked phone calls must have been a success after all. Penny was a junkie I had met once or twice before who adamantly proclaimed that the song "Penny Lane" was written about her. She worked for Jerry at The Telesis Foundation, the outpatient detox center where Jennifer and I used to get our meds. Jerry was an old junkie who ran the outpatient center and he had a huge heart. He'd sent Penny to speak on my behalf. Maybe she felt sorry for me. Maybe it was some kind of code between junkies, wanting to look out for someone and something she recognized so well. She did a great job at making my case, and not a word of it was true.

"Mr. Rafati's been doing great," she said. "He's been attending outpatient meetings, he's been drug tested regularly, and he is an active part of the community. He unfortunately had a slip and we really believe he deserves another chance."

The judge asked a few more questions and Penny told a few more lies.

Then the judge said to Penny, "Based on what you've told me, I feel it would be appropriate to release Mr. Rafati into your custody and back into your program. Are you willing to do that? Are you willing to take him back into your program?"

"Yes, of course," Penny said.

I couldn't believe what was happening. Were they really releasing me?

Then my hero of a public defender stood up and pointed at the bright yellow jumpsuit I was wearing, which the jail gave to everyone inside the Pill Pod.

"Mr. Rafati is not fit to be released into the general public," he declared.

The judge considered me for a few moments as I held my breath.

"Let's get him psychologically evaluated," she said.

I had to get back on that bus, but this time I had hope. I got psychologically evaluated by the LA County Jail psychiatrist—three hours of the strangest questions I'd ever heard—and they declared me fit for release.

I was free.

* * *

When I got out of Los Angeles County Jail, I temporarily resurfaced into society. Aside from scaring the shit out of me, jail also did me some good physically. I'd put on about 20 pounds and had started to resemble a human being again.

I called my buddy Duane, who wasn't exactly homeless, but definitely couch surfing. In jail I had made countless pacts with God that if I could just get out of there, I would never drink or use again and in those moments I meant them, but my, how things changed once I saw daylight. There was no fucking way I was gonna go to AA—that was for losers. And to make a point, I began periodically having beers, but never more than one, to prove to myself and everybody else that there was no fucking way that I was an alcoholic.

One evening a couple months later we were at a seafood restaurant and I was having my routine beer. Duane ordered a Jack and Coke, but only finished half of it because a girl he had been talking to wanted to leave. I was jealous and resentful because 1) nobody wanted to leave with me and 2) I had no ride back to the house where we were crashing. I grabbed his Jack and Coke and chugged it. Within seconds of that hard alcohol hitting my stomach, I felt a warmth and then a hunger. A hunger for drugs and destruction. A hunger for oblivion. I don't know how this shit happens, but it always does—out of the corner of my eye I saw the local coke dealer, Christian. You couldn't miss the guy because he actually walked around with a briefcase that was full of drugs (again, only in Malibu...).

I walked up to him and I didn't ask for a gram, I *demanded* it. He asked me for the money and my response was, "I'll get you the fucking money later. Just give me a gram."

I had done some deals with him in the past and I had never burned him, so I guess he figured I was good for the money. I followed him into the bathroom and as soon as he began to reach his hand toward me to give me the gram, I quickly snatched it and ran. I literally *ran* out of the restaurant, through the parking lot, and down Pacific Coast Highway to Greg's house. Greg was an older crackhead who had a tiny apartment on the beach where I used to occasionally stop by and smoke crack. Greg had a couple of dirty secrets that he had shared with me on one of the long nights we'd spent together after everyone else at the party had disappeared: 1) he shot up just like I did but didn't want anyone to know, so he hid needles inside of an old radio in his bathroom and 2) he had Hepatitis C.

I arrived at Greg's house panting, completely out of breath, and started pounding on his gate, although I'm not sure why I bothered because I didn't even wait for him to answer. I jumped over the gate effortlessly, with a strength that surprised even me. I ran down the stairs and up to his door and began pounding again. This time I waited about 20 seconds before pulling my sleeve over my hand and punching through the window to open the door from the inside. I didn't even look around when I ran into the apartment. I just went straight to the bathroom, reached above the cabinet, and grabbed that old radio full of dirty, old, used needles and began shooting all the coke into my arm.

I'd like to say it was a gradual descent back into hell, but I returned instantaneously into the psychotic and paranoid state, wanting nothing but oblivion. I couldn't bear being myself, not even for a moment. The shame was too much, the fear, the guilt. I just couldn't take it. I disappeared back into the crack houses and shooting galleries, back into the homeless abyss. It was in those first few weeks that I found myself on a bus heading toward downtown LA. The bus was empty except for two other poor, unfortunate souls.

"Where is everybody?" I asked the bus driver.

He looked in the rearview mirror but didn't answer.

When I finally made it downtown, the streets were empty. *What the fuck's going on?*

I had this eerie, cold feeling inside of me. Was this the apocalypse or something?

I finally saw a familiar face, an older black woman named LaWanda who was in a wheelchair—a dope fiend just like I was, but a saint of a woman. She had helped me out several times before when I was dopesick, sharing with me what little she had left.

"You okay, baby?" she asked.

"No, I'm sick. I'm sick, LaWanda. What the fuck is going on? I need to get some shit."

She said, "Baby, you know ain't nobody out here today."

"What do you mean? I don't understand."

"Baby, don't you know?"

"Know what? *Please,* I'm fucking sick."

"Oh, baby, come here," she said as she took my hand. She looked up at me with those kind brown eyes of hers and squeezed my hand tightly. "Today is Christmas."

I was dumbfounded. I couldn't breathe for a moment. I could hear the faraway laughter of that old man: "There's no Christmas for junkies."

I broke down and I cried. I sobbed. I knelt down and bent over LaWanda's wheelchair and she held onto me. She kept trying to tell me that if we could get up to San Julian we could get some shit, but I ignored her and just kept crying.

What the fuck happened to my life? How could this happen? How, if there's a fucking God in heaven, could I end up like this?

I pushed LaWanda in her wheelchair all the way up to San Julian, also known as Skid Row. We went tent to tent, asking people if they could spare a balloon. We eventually found somebody who was holding and I "got well."

The following day, I panhandled for some change and took a bus to the welfare office on Pico Blvd. It took about six hours to stand in line and fill out all the paperwork, but by late afternoon, I had $212 in food stamp vouchers, hotel vouchers, and bus tokens. I took the bus back downtown to the check cashing place to get my food stamps, which I quickly traded for drugs. I still had good enough negotiating skills to get a large amount at near wholesale cost.

My appetite, however, was insatiable. I quickly shot and smoked everything I had bought, so I went panhandling for more money. The moment I got enough, I ran and bought more drugs. I didn't have it in me to harm or rob anybody, but I did anything else I could for drugs or money to buy drugs.

Late one night, I was somewhere deep in Hollywood

when I ran out of crack and no one was around to pan-handle off of. I went back to one of the dealers on Orange Avenue and begged him for more. I know it sounds crazy, but sometimes that actually worked. They would get bored standing out there all night and sometimes if you just hung out and talked with them, they would give you free hits. This guy didn't want to talk. He asked me to come into the alley with him. He wanted me to blow him but I refused. Then he asked me if he could play with my feet.

"Are you gonna give me some crack?" I asked, and he handed me a $20 rock.

I couldn't believe it. I shoved the whole thing in the pipe, took a massive hit, and blew out a big white ghost. It was a real bell-ringer. My heart raced. He kept rubbing my feet. I asked him for another hit.

He said "Hang on" and undid his pants. He pulled out his dick and then handed me another $20 rock. He started jacking off. And I smoked the crack. He kept jacking off and handing me crack and I just kept smoking it and smoking it.

It certainly wasn't in my game plan when I left Ohio and drove across the country in search of fortune and fame to wind up at 4:00 a.m. in a dark alley with a homeless black crack dealer jacking himself off while playing with my feet.

My mother was the only person left who would still take my phone calls. When I ran out of food stamps or hotel vouchers or simply didn't have the hustle left in me to pan-handle, I would call her and beg for money. Usually crying and pleading worked, but if not, I could always threaten to kill myself.

The last conversation I had with my mother during that time started out pretty typical. I called her collect from Santa

Monica. I had no patience to beg or plead that day, so I went right into the whole "I'm gonna kill myself" part. My poor mother. She could barely afford to feed herself and here I was, yet again, screaming at her to send me money for drugs. I had convinced myself that it was her fault that I was in this position, that she owed me for not being there when I had needed her most.

I didn't tell her the money was for drugs, but she knew. She broke down crying. Before she hung up she said, "I'm going to send you money this one last time, but don't ever, ever call me again. I mean it this time. I won't answer."

I was too manic to care. As soon as I got the money, I bought some heroin. Now I just needed some coke to go along with it. I called a Jamaican coke dealer I knew. He met me in an alley over by the McDonald's on Second Street in Santa Monica. As soon as I got in his car he said, "Goddamn, mon, you smell."

"I'm sorry."

"No, mon, what's going on?" he asked. "You haven't changed your clothes for a while?"

"Look, I just want to get some stuff, can you please just..."

"Where are you staying?"

I wasn't staying anywhere. I slept wherever I wound up, sometimes in cheap hotels but mostly on the streets and under the bridge with the crackheads. But I wanted to get back to Malibu. I knew some girls whose family rented an old house up in the hills. They were these old hippies who took a liking to me and really enjoyed the music that Duane and I had made together. The dad was from England and the mom grew up in San Francisco during the '60s. They had seven daughters. There was a shack in the back of their property that I'd stayed in from time to time before I'd gone off the deep end. It had no running water or electricity, but I ran an extension cord from the neighbor's house and went to the bathroom out back in the woods. The entire property was really run down, but there was so much love in that family it didn't seem to matter. The daughters all loved me and they would bring me food and sometimes even make me cookies. I felt safe there.

So I told the coke dealer, "I'm staying in Malibu, up Winding Way."

"I'll give you a ride."

He rolled down the windows and drove me all the way from Santa Monica to Malibu, about 20 miles. I couldn't understand what he was doing. Why would he drive me all the way out to Malibu? At first I thought he was trying to kill me, but then he started going on and on, in that heavy Jamaican accent of his, about how I needed to get my life together.

We got to Winding Way West and he took a right on the street. Just to be safe, I didn't want him to know where I was staying so before we got to the property I said, "Here, right here is good."

"Are you sure?"

"Yeah, right here is fine."

I pulled out the money that my mom had sent me and went to hand him a hundred dollar bill for the coke. He just stared at me.

"Put your money away, mon," he said. "And do me a favor. Get some help. Take a shower and get some help, mon."

I was a little thrown off by the comment. How bad off do you have to be for your coke dealer to beg you to get help and refuse your money? As I got out of the car, he reached over and grabbed me sternly and said, "And don't ever fucking call me again, mon."

Fuck him! I thought as I walked away. But then a strange feeling came over me—one I couldn't really describe other than by saying that the monsters or demons that had hijacked my soul were starving for what I had in my pocket and a hunger overtook me like something I'd never felt before. I wasn't far from the property and the safety of that shack, but I simply couldn't wait. I stopped in front of a house with a light on in front of their gate.

I pulled out my massive spoon and dumped as much of the coke as I could fit, lightly cooked it, and drew it all up into one of my big 27-gauge intramuscular syringes and shot half the syringe into my arm. But I didn't taste anything. For people who have never shot cocaine before, especially coke coming from Mexico, as soon as you boot it into your arm there's a syrupy kerosene or gasoline taste that drips from your gums and you can sort of gauge how hard it's gonna hit you.

But I tasted nothing. So I pushed the rest of the syringe into my arm. Before the plunger found its final resting stop, the initial blast of cocaine hit me like a shovel on the back of the head. And now the rest was seconds away from hitting as well. In a split second, I remembered the Jamaicans always had the really pure stuff that came through Florida and up I-75. It wasn't washed with kerosene or gasoline, like the Mexican coke was, and it didn't have much of a taste when you pushed off. But it was strong. It was *fucking* strong.

As all this was running through my head, I heard the sound of sirens. The last thing I remember seeing as I grabbed my chest and looked up in horror was a security camera up above the gate, with its red light blinking. I tried to run but my legs folded underneath me like jelly. They were useless. I gasped for air but couldn't get a breath. Sweat poured from my head and my face. I tried again to breathe but couldn't. The sirens were getting louder and louder.

Finally—*gasp*—a half a breath. I came up on one leg and fell straight down on my face. I fumbled around desperately with my hands and arms, the only things that seemed to be working. I couldn't see; my vision was completely gone.

Gasp—another half a breath. I got halfway up this time. There was a shooting pain in my chest. My whole body was ice cold. I could feel a seizure coming. I dove, somehow, with all of my strength and started rolling, falling rather, down a hill into a gully. The sirens were now screaming and I could hear the screeching of tires as they made their way up Winding Way West.

I pulled some leaves and twigs, anything within arm's reach, over me. I still couldn't see anything. I buried myself beneath the dirt and old rotten leaves and sticks and then I froze as I heard the cop cars pulling up and parking.

I lay there for hours, blind and paralyzed. They must've walked past me 20 times. A few times I could even feel the pressure of their footsteps as the leaves and twigs crunched under their feet. It felt like an elephant was sitting on my chest. Bugs began to crawl on me—slugs and ants and centipedes. They crawled on my arms. They crawled on my face. Inside my ears. Inside my nose. Just like the leaves and twigs, I was rotting. I was decomposing—a ball of filth. The bugs and the earth made their move to consume me. And I let them. I didn't dare move. I had no right. I deserved to rot and decompose in that dirt, under those rotten leaves. I had no other choice. I had nowhere to go, no one to call, no one to co-sign my behavior or enable me. I had burned every bridge that I had ever known. My own mother wouldn't take my calls. Fuck, my *coke dealer* wouldn't take my calls. Every time I had hit bottom before, I'd grabbed a shovel and had kept digging. This time there was nowhere left to dig.

I surrendered to my fate and became one with the dirt and the filth. It was over. I was dead.

A stillness and calm overtook me. My breath evened out and returned to normal. I heard a familiar sound that I had not heard or paid attention to for decades—it was the sound of the birds waking up. One by one, slowly but surely, their beautiful, quiet song broke into a symphony.

I started to pray, asking God for forgiveness. With the sound of the birds, a fragment of hope entered my soul. If I could just see again, if I could just walk again, I would change. I prayed harder and harder and the birds chirped louder and louder and I could tell it was getting light out.

"God, please, please, please. I don't want to do this anymore. I *can't* do this anymore. Please just let me see again, please let me walk again, please don't let me go to jail. I swear I will never drink or get high again. Please just let me get out of this and let me get my vision back and let me be able to walk again and I will never *ever* do it again."

This time I meant it. I could not go on. I didn't have it in me to continue the way I was existing—I couldn't even call it living. If I had to keep existing this way, I would rather die in that ditch.

✳ ✳ ✳

My vision returned somewhat, but only a little and very slowly. I checked to see if my legs moved. They did, but not completely. I sat up and brushed the leaves and the dirt and the bugs off of me. And with blurred vision and wobbly legs, I half walked, half crawled the rest of the way to the shack.

I slept for a day and a half. When I woke up the following afternoon, I went to the main house and asked if I could use their phone. Surprisingly, the family didn't really react to my being there. I had stumbled to that shack in pretty bad condition before and I suppose they saw it coming.

I called Jerry, the owner of the Telesis Foundation, because he now owned a fancy rehab in Malibu called Malibu Ranch.

I begged him, "Can I please come to your rehab?"

"No way," he replied. "Not if you still look like you did the last time I saw you. I can't have you at my place."

I cried and I begged.

"No," he said. "I'm sorry."

Next I tried Penny.

"Can I please come over? I'm done. I swear to God I'm done. I'll never get high again, I swear to God. Please just let me come over and stay at your place for a month and get a job."

She said, "No, I can't." I thought she'd hung up, then I heard her voice again: "But I'll call Bob Forrest for you."

"Anybody," I said, "anything, please."

She called Bob Forrest, who worked for a charity called MAP, the Musicians Assistance Program, or in my case, Failed Musicians Assistance Program. It was a program for anyone in the music industry who needed help with addiction.

Bob graciously agreed and I called him to get the address. "Yeah, just get a ride down here and we'll take care of you, man. Don't worry about it."

I was crying. "I don't have any money. I don't have any family."

"Just get down here," he said. "We'll take care of you."

I showered in the main house and borrowed some clothes from one of the older girls to take with me—jeans, sweatpants, flip flops, a couple of old concert tees, and a nice, big, comfortable, warm sweatshirt. By the time I got to MAP, I was in bad shape from withdrawal. I had to interview with the head guy, a famous old jazz musician and ex-dope fiend named Buddy Arnold. He hated me at first sight—maybe it was the bleached blond hair, or what was left of it, anyway.

"No way," he said immediately. "There's nothing we can do. You're not a published musician."

Bob kept saying, "Come on, Buddy, we got to help him. We got to help him."

Buddy told me four or five more times to leave his office.

"I don't have anywhere to go," I said, sobbing. "Please, please help me."

Finally, just to get me to shut up, he said, "Okay, fine. I'm going to help you and I know I'm going to regret it."

Bob drove me to Pasadena Recovery Center. It was June 15th, 2003. When I got there they gave me some pills and I slept for three days straight. When I woke up I was alone in my room. I knew exactly what was going on and where I was. Tears rolled down my face yet again. I closed the door to my room, knelt next to the bed, folded my hands, and prayed.

"Whatever you are, if you're there, please take this hell away from me."

I will never forget those words as long as I live. I felt a lifting. The nausea and exhaustion remained, but a little bit of levity came into my being. I asked God for help and God answered immediately with an overwhelming feeling of, "You're going to be okay."

I didn't see any burning bush and no angels came out of the sky to wipe the sweat from my forehead. I didn't need any of that. The feeling of lightness, a feeling of knowing that there was a God and that God was going to take care of me, that was all I needed.

When I finally left my room, I was approached by the psychiatrist, who had an entire medication program set up for me. They wanted to put me on Lexapro, Wellbutrin, Trazodone and Seroquel. I'd been on all of these at one time or another during my brief periods of abstinence from drugs and alcohol and knew how effective they were.

"No," I said. "Not this time. I don't want anything."

"Are you sure?" the doctor asked. "Because you'll be going through withdrawal for quite a while."

"I don't care. I don't want anything."

They even offered me Clonidine, the high blood pressure patch that Dr. Waldman had given me when I'd broken into Exodus rehab during my first major withdrawal.

"No," I said. "I don't want any medication. I don't want any antidepressants. I want to face this once and for all."

June 18th, 2003 was my last day of taking any type of drink or drug. The two and a half weeks that followed were the hardest weeks of my life. I didn't sleep. I would nod off for 20 minutes here and there, only to have night terrors, sleep paralysis, and hallucinations. I was covered in abscesses. I turned shades of green and yellow that I'd never seen on a human being. Bright yellow bile came out of both ends of me for days. Every time I tried to eat, I threw up. My skin crawled, my bones ached, I felt like I was 100 years old and none of it seemed like it was ever going to get better. It was fucking hell.

But even in that condition, I was a thousand times better off than I had been two weeks earlier. I drank gallons of coffee and smoked copious amounts of cigarettes. I shared a lot of the horror stories of my drinking and using, but people weren't grossed out or offended in the slightest. In fact, they laughed. They *really* laughed. And I laughed with them. The scarier or the more disgusting the stories, the harder we laughed. Deep, belly-aching laughter. It had been years since I'd laughed like that and it felt so good.

CHAPTER SEVEN

AS THE END OF MY 30 DAYS AT PASADENA RECOVERY CENTER began to draw near, I was forced to consider where I would go next. I knew that if I went back to Malibu, back to that shack, and back to all my old friends who were still getting high, I would slip right back into the abyss. I had never thought I'd be in this position—I didn't want to leave rehab. I wasn't buying the whole AA or NA thing, not by any stretch of the imagination, but I loved having a roof over my head and a bed to sleep in and food to eat. Most of all, I loved feeling safe for the first time in a really, *really* long time. So I came up with a plan.

When Bob Forrest showed up the next day, I told him my brilliant idea. I would simply stay. I had become pretty good at sweeping, mopping, and cleaning because they made us do chores there. At first I fucking hated it, but after a while I found great solace in the work. It did something for me. In hindsight, I think it began to clean my soul a little, and Lord knows it was filthy. I asked Bob if I could stay at Pasadena Recovery Center and be a janitor in exchange for room and board.

He laughed hysterically. "No, buddy. I'm gonna talk to MAP about putting you in sober living."

"Like, a halfway house?" I said, not even trying to disguise the disgust in my voice. "That's for fucking losers."

He laughed even harder. "Well, you might be right, and that's why you're going there."

Bob and I took a long drive that afternoon. He took me to Starbucks and bought me a venti Frappuccino. On the drive back, I was so jacked on sugar and caffeine that I spoke incessantly. Bob couldn't get a word in. I didn't pay attention to where he was driving. The van stopped abruptly and Bob said, "C'mon, man. Hop out. I'm gonna show you your sober living."

What the fuck is he talking about? We were in some weird grassy area full of hills. I kept talking as I followed Bob, paying no attention to anything but myself. It seems so crazy to me now that I didn't realize where I was. Bob stopped suddenly and pointed down at the ground. "Here it is, man," he said in that twangy old voice of his. "Here's your sober living."

I looked down and saw a headstone. It said "Hillel Slovak 1962-1988."

"Who's this?" I asked.

"This was my best friend and he didn't wanna go to sober living either. He had everything that you say you want—money, fame, a music career, girls—and this is where he is. In a fucking graveyard. And this is where you're gonna be if you don't go to sober living."

We walked back to the van without saying a word to one another. Finally, I said, "Okay. I'll go to sober living."

Bob remained silent.

"I'm gonna go to Genesis House, right?"

Genesis House was the cool sober living in Cheviot Hills, where all of the real musicians went.

"No," Bob replied angrily. "You're not going to Genesis House. You'll go where I say you're gonna go." I had never seen Bob mad before.

Bob had just the place for me. It was called New Perceptions. A black-owned and black-operated sober living deep in the heart of the San Fernando Valley. It was owned by a woman named Thelma and her brother Will. They had both grown up in South Central Los Angeles.

I checked in with Thelma, who reminded me of The Oracle from *The Matrix*. She had been sober for decades and carried an aura of calm wisdom. She introduced me to Will and, while he and I were talking, I couldn't help but stare at this weird scar on his neck, wondering where it had come from.

Finally, he said, "You're looking at my neck, right?"

"What? No, no, no. I was just, well, yeah."

He pointed at the scar. "It's from when a dude shot me."

"You got shot in the neck?"

"Yeah."

I couldn't help myself. "Why did you get shot in the neck?"

"Oh, because I shot some other dudes and then they shot me."

Even with everything I'd been through, I thought, *What the fuck? How did I get here?*

I wanted to get high all day, every day, but I didn't. Instead, my time was spent sweating, chain-smoking, and drinking exceptionally bad coffee. MAP gave all of us $40 a week to live on, and the first thing I did was make sure I had enough cigarettes for the week. Once that was settled, I spent the rest on Ramen noodles and a big box of pasta and tomato sauce.

And that's how the other clients and I lived. We used a lot of irreverent, inappropriate humor to make it through the day. Nothing was off limits; nothing was sacred. And again, the more inappropriate the joke, the harder we laughed. The other guys made fun of me for being an Arab-Polack, then we all made fun of the Jewish guy, then the black guy, until everybody got a turn.

Every now and then, an eerie silence would set in and one of us would just blurt it out: "Fuck, man. I wanna get high so bad." And then everybody would crack up laughing because they were all thinking the exact same thing. But no one got high. Bob took all of the worst cases—the guys who absolutely, positively wouldn't make it—and he stuck us all together under one roof and somehow it just worked. We were all so happy just to be alive.

When I was alone I struggled with that. Being alive. I shouldn't have survived the places and positions I'd put myself in. Most people don't. Why had I? It certainly doesn't have anything to do with being tougher or stronger because, trust me, many, many people who were stronger and tougher than I am didn't make it. Too many people who were smarter than I am, kinder than I am, and just better human beings than I am died. And I don't know why. To this day, I don't know why. I still wrestle with guilt and confusion about it sometimes.

The sober living made us go to two recovery meetings every day. I fucking hated them but I went. If I didn't go, they would kick me out, and I didn't want to disappoint Bob Forrest. So I went, usually with a guy named Frank Violence from the sober living. We gave him endless shit about his name because the only fistfight he'd ever gotten into was with his girlfriend right before he went to jail and rehab, and she'd won. She'd stabbed him in the face with her car keys, beaten the shit out of him, and left him for dead in a phone booth.

I went to the meetings but I wouldn't go inside. I stood outside and smoked the whole time while I tried to pick up girls who were doing the same thing. The first meeting I actually went inside for was on Third and Gardner St. and I gotta be honest—the only reason I walked in was because I saw a guy who was the lead singer of a band that I really loved walking into the meeting, as well as a bunch of really cute girls. So it was the grace of God that got me sober, but it was my ego and hormones that got me into 12-step programs.

The meetings started to grow on me. The more I went, the better I felt. Eventually I started to listen, pay attention, and I heard little pearls of wisdom that carried me through the days. I still wanted to get high and I hated sleeping in a room with three other guys snoring, burping, and farting all night but it beat the shit out of living on the streets.

Then somebody took me to get my first AIDS test.

* * *

I'd been sober for three months. One of the managers at Thelma and Will's place was this kid who had tattoos everywhere, even crawling up his neck. He freaked me out. He was driving both of us to a 12-step meeting on a Wednesday when he asked me, "Have you ever been tested before?"

I felt short of breath and started squirming in my seat. I'd never been tested, even after sharing needles with someone I knew had AIDS.

"Yeah," I lied. "Yeah, of course."

"And you're clean?"

"Yeah, yeah. Nothing."

"You don't even have Hep C?" he asked.

"Nope." The sad truth is that I looked like I had Hepatitis C, AIDS, and God knows what else. I was horribly skinny, dehydrated from all the cigarettes and coffee, malnourished from eating nothing but Ramen and spaghetti with cheap tomato sauce, and I had weird splotches all over my face. People asked me all the time if I was feeling okay, if I was unwell.

We drove in silence for a few miles, then he asked, "Do you want to get tested again?"

I said, "No, no. I don't need to."

"When's the last time you got tested?"

"They tested me in rehab," I said. Another lie.

"Well, you know, you've got to get tested every six months. It has an incubation period."

Shit.

"All right," I said. "Yeah, I'll get tested again when I get a chance."

As I was talking he pulled into a parking lot. We weren't at the meeting.

"What are you doing?" I said.

"You can get tested right here."

"Oh. Yeah, I don't have any money for that."

"It's free."

It was the Tarzana Treatment Center. They had a mobile unit on site twice a week, on Wednesdays and Fridays, that offered free testing. Yet again, I was too proud to back down.

"Come on, man," he said. "Let's go do this."

I nodded and smiled. "Yeah, cool. Let's do this."

I felt a wave of panic wash over me. I felt like running, but I knew that wouldn't change anything. Deep down I felt I had something terrible from all the things I'd done. Memories started flashing through my mind of the times I'd intentionally shot way too much coke or heroin, secretly hoping I would die painlessly, before I started wasting away.

I went in the trailer and a nurse drew my blood and asked me questions about sharing needles, anal sex, all kinds of weird shit. She made notes and then did strange things to the blood they'd taken. As I sat there waiting, I tried to prepare myself for the bad news. Which one did I have? Both?

Then she told me the results would be back in a week.

Fuck, a week? How was I supposed to make it through an entire week with this shit hanging over me? For the next six days I couldn't eat. I couldn't sleep. I smoked so much I should have just eaten the cigarettes.

Wednesday morning arrived like some unwanted guest. The mobile unit wouldn't be open until 3:00 p.m. and the trip loomed over me all day. Around 1:30 p.m., feeling as though I couldn't take another minute of waiting, I threw myself on my bed and tried to force myself to relax. I passed out.

When I woke up it was dark outside. I jumped up out of bed and ran around the house trying to find a ride to the clinic. Too late. No one could take me and the clinic was closed anyway. I'd missed my results. I had to wait another two days. Two more days of hell.

Friday finally came and I made it to the clinic. The lab technician who was helping me was very nonchalant, which freaked me out even more. I just wanted to know what I had, how I was going to die, and this dude couldn't care less. I was shaking and sweating as I tapped my feet nervously.

The tech stopped what he was doing and watched me for a few seconds. "Hey, man, you might want to think about getting clean."

"What?" I was so wound-up, I figured I hadn't heard him correctly.

"You should stop using. You should get clean."

"What the fuck are you talking about? I'm clean three and a half months."

He looked skeptical. "*You're* clean and sober?"

"Yeah, I'm fucking sober. Why?"

"Well...you look pretty rough."

"Thanks."

"Why are you shaking?" he asked.

"I'm waiting for you to give me my fucking test results!"

He leaned back in his chair and replied, "Oh, you're fine. We would've told you if something was wrong."

I fell to the ground. I curled up into the fetal position and sobbed. The tech came over and helped me back into my chair.

"I'm sorry. I shouldn't have said you looked rough."

"No, no, no. I don't care. I *do* look rough. I don't care. Oh, my God. I don't have AIDS. I don't have AIDS! I don't—wait, what about Hep C?"

"Oh, we didn't do that test. You have to do a separate test for that."

Of course. But at that point, I didn't even care. I thought, *Let me have Hep C. As long as I don't have AIDS. I don't care.*

I was so happy that I wasn't going to rot away in a hospital bed.

* * *

I stayed at the sober living for several months, which probably saved my life. When the money from MAP ran out, I
called around to see if anyone had a place where I could stay.
I wasn't having any luck, but I didn't let that discourage me.
I was just looking forward to getting out of sober living and
having my freedom back. I ended up staying with a giant
biker friend named Baron, who agreed to let me live at his
place as long as I stayed sober, went to two meetings a day,
did chores, and got a sponsor.

Freedom, huh? It turned out that staying at Baron's
was tougher than staying at sober living. He had gotten
sober a couple of years earlier and was absolutely vigilant
about recovery.

I did everything he asked of me. I got a sponsor, Robbie,
who was incredibly kind to me. He bought me a cell phone
and my first pair of new shoes in years, and with his help
I started going through the 12 steps. I learned that addicts
typically have something they are "using at." It might be
their father, an uncle who molested them, or just a really
horrible childhood in general. Alcoholics and drug addicts
are damaged, so they seek the drink and the drug to cope
with the pain.

My shit was abandonment. My mother had abandoned
me when I was a child. She didn't protect me when I needed
her to. My girlfriend Kim broke up with me in grade school
for no apparent reason. My girlfriend Kori transferred to a
different high school. My other high school girlfriend, Jamie,
broke up with me and moved away. Claudia left me. Anna
left me. And Jennifer, my last girlfriend and drug buddy who

was never going to leave me? Gone.

Robbie made me write down the names of all of the people who had abandoned me and what our relationships were like. The pain was overwhelming as I reminisced about how unlovable I was and how everybody who'd said they'd loved me and had promised they would never leave me had always left me. Me, me, me—I was so sad for me. When I was done Robbie read through the list.

"Well, what was your part in this?" he asked.

"My part? Nothing. They fucking abandoned me."

"But what was your part? How did you contribute to that?"

"I didn't fucking contribute to anything," I said. "I had a mom who abandoned me, so I attracted these girls into my life who abandoned me, and that's it."

"So you didn't have any part in it?"

"No, I didn't have any fucking part in it!" I yelled.

Robbie smiled. "Did you ever yell at them?"

"Yell at them?" I thought about it. "Yeah, of course I yelled at them."

"Did you ever swear at them?"

"Yes, I fucking swore at them."

He nodded. "Did you ever hit them?"

"No," I said. "I mean, not really. I got into some altercations with them, but I never, like, punched them in the face."

"That's not what I'm asking," Robbie said. "Did you ever hit them? Did you ever push them?"

"Yeah, I probably pushed them."

"All of them?" he asked.

"I don't fucking know. Yeah, I pushed them in an argument or, you know, yeah, maybe I slapped a couple of them once or twice."

"Really?"

"Yeah, why?"

"Just asking. Write it down. Did you ever cheat on any of them?"

"Yeah, of course I cheated. I cheated on all of them."

Robbie looked shocked. "*All* of them?"

"Yeah, why? Does that surprise you? That's what guys do."

"It is?"

"Yes," I said, "men cheat. That's what they fucking do. Men cheat. All men cheat."

"So you know all men? You know all three billion men on the planet?"

"Dude, I know enough fucking guys to know what guys do. Guys cheat."

Robbie leaned in close to me. "Khalil, I've got to tell you something, and I need you to really listen to me."

"Sure, what is it?"

He tapped the list. "These girls didn't abandon you."

"The fuck they didn't," I said.

He shook his head. "They didn't abandon you. They *escaped*."

I was speechless.

Robbie continued, "If you love someone like you claim you loved them—and I'm not gonna debate whether you did or you didn't—but if you love someone, you don't cheat on them, you don't scream at them, you don't call them names, you don't push them, you don't slap them. You mistreated these girls to the point where they couldn't take it anymore and they escaped. Do me a favor. In the future, when you feel that you really care about somebody, don't do that stuff. Don't yell at them, don't call them names, don't cheat on them."

I broke down and cried. I cried over all the terrible things I had done to the people I loved. I cried because I could see everything so clearly now. Growing up I thought everyone else had a perfect life except for me. I sought that perfection within my relationships with women, but at the slightest bit of discomfort, I would self-sabotage because I didn't know how to put an end to things with dignity and grace. I was always running. I was just running. And really I was just running from my own shadow.

That realization was a powerful turning point in my life. I could feel the burden of my depression and anxiety lightening. Thank you, Robbie.

Soon after, I called my mom and started asking questions about her past. I had no idea about the work camps and everything she had gone through during the war. She didn't share much with me, just bits and pieces, but it was enough for me to realize that this woman had done the best she could given her circumstances—the trauma, the violent monster of a husband, and me, the pain in the ass son. It wasn't her fault I'd wound up a broke and homeless junkie. It was mine.

My whole world began to unravel.

✳ ✳ ✳

Robbie bought me a gym membership at Spectrum in Pacific Palisades and I started working out pretty regularly. It was brutal at first, but I forced myself to go every day. They had a sauna there that was balls hot and I really got into it. I would do a sauna every day, 15-20 minute intervals, with an ice cold shower in between. I became obsessed, spending two hours at a time doing this routine. Someone at the gym asked me if I had ever tried Niacin before. I said no, then immediately drove to the health food store, bought some, and came back. The first time I tried it, I took a couple hundred milligrams and almost wound up in the emergency room. I didn't know that you had to gradually build your way up.

I bought myself a dry brush with bristles made of boar's hair. It hurt like hell, especially in combination with the flushing and itching caused by the Niacin, but I could literally see myself looking better, looking younger each day that went by. I found something very cathartic and meditative about the whole detoxification process. As I scrubbed my bare skin with those harsh boar's hair bristles, I wasn't just cleaning away dead skin or draining my lymphatic system—I was scrubbing my soul. I wanted to burn off, scrub off, and drain all of the filth and sin I had accumulated.

I met a beautiful girl there who taught Pilates and eventually asked her out on a date. Much to my surprise, things went incredibly well and progressed quickly. I was completely open and honest with her about my past. Not surprisingly, she said she didn't feel comfortable sleeping with me until I got tested for everything.

Everything...fuck.

I figured this was the part where I learned that I had Hepatitis C and had to tell her and she would dump me. I went home and told Robbie about my dilemma. I was frantic and wanted to get tested immediately and I didn't want to have to wait around for the results. I had done that once before and it was hell.

"Take it easy," Robbie said. "You don't need to wait a week."

Robbie had a best friend who was a porn producer in the

San Fernando Valley. We called him together and he gave me the name of a clinic.

"Go there and tell them you work for me. Tell them that you're a new porn star and you're gonna shoot a film. Make up a porn name. You'll have your test results back in 24 hours. Easy."

"Is that even possible?" I asked.

"Yeah, it's the most accurate test out there. They do DNA testing. They can tell if you have Hep C, HIV, even if there's something dormant in your system."

The clinic was on Ventura Boulevard in the San Fernando Valley. It wasn't quite like he'd said it would be. I couldn't just go in and tell them I was going to shoot some porn and needed a test. This place was a non-profit charity for people in the porn industry and was set up by some beautiful woman who had unknowingly acquired HIV through her work. There was a lengthy process you had to go through and they asked me a bunch of questions:

"Which producer are you working for?"

"What's the name of the film?"

"Is it gay, straight, or bi?"

"Are you doing anal?"

I sat there for three hours with all these young men and women who were about to *actually* do porn for the first time. We watched videos about enemas, feces, seminal fluid, and what the AIDS virus and Hepatitis C are like. It was surreal.

Robbie's friend was right about one thing: I got the results back the next day. I had no Hepatitis C and a 100% guarantee that I had no HIV because I was past the incubation period.

I went out with the Pilates instructor and showed her the results. I was very happy. Because I was clean and for other reasons...I'm sure you can imagine.

❋ ❋ ❋

I was sitting in Marmalade Café in Malibu, nine months sober, when I got a phone call from my mom. She sounded incredibly distraught. She had just left the doctor's office and had been diagnosed with cancer. I was blindsided.

It killed me that I didn't have the money to go home and visit her or help her with medical bills. She was 66 years old, alone, and still working six days a week as a nurse's assistant at Toledo Hospital. She lived paycheck to paycheck in a tiny apartment in Kenwood Gardens, which was one step up from a housing project.

As soon as I hung up the phone, I made a decision: I was going to make money. I was going to be able to take care of my mom. That was my only goal. I had thrown my life away, taken it for granted, and I probably didn't deserve to make money, but there was nothing that was going to stop me from being able to take care of my mom.

❋ ❋ ❋

I kept going to the 12-step meetings and grew a deep appreciation for the unconditional love and support they provided. Where else can you walk in, raise your hand, and say, "This one time I ran out of coke so I bought crack and broke it down with lemon juice and shot it into my neck," then have complete strangers clap for you, give you hugs, and invite you to dinner? Eventually I even started following the advice and wisdom the meetings offered, which included having the humility to tell people I needed work. It didn't matter what it was; I would do it.

I met this really sweet gay couple named Chris and Glen who let me clean their house. Another person suggested I go meet a woman named Sherman, who was a dog groomer, and she gave me $20 a day to wash dogs and squeeze their anal glands. I hadn't even known dogs *had* anal glands but apparently they did and they needed to be squeezed.

Somebody else introduced me to a handyman and construction worker named Daryl Cobb who took me to work with him, removing a tree stump with a pick axe and shovel. It was brutal. I lasted about 10 minutes before I broke down and started sobbing. Daryl was an incredibly wise and compassionate man. He spoke to me at great length about his own sobriety, which was something like 16 or 17 years. I couldn't believe it—how could someone stay sober that long?

I worked the rest of the day doing tasks that were less physically demanding. And as the sun set, we drove back to Malibu and he dropped me off in front of the Starbucks. As I was getting out of his truck, he handed me a hundred dollar bill. It was the most money I'd held since getting sober.

I took the cash and went straight to Malibu Kitchen and ordered tuna with Swiss on a toasted, seeded baguette. I can still see and smell that sandwich like it's right in front of my face. My teeth were falling apart and I could only chew on one side of my mouth so I had to be careful, which was challenging because this was the greatest sandwich I had ever had in my life. As I took in the aroma of the tuna and freshly baked bread, tears welled up in my eyes. It felt so good to put in an honest day's work and earn that food. I hadn't begged for it or sold drugs to get the cash to buy it or used food stamps. I'd worked for it. I wanted to keep doing that. I didn't know it at the time, but that moment was the pivotal point where I broke the cycle of learned helplessness.

One day I was washing dogs at Sherman's when a big, tall black man pulled up in a Rolls Royce and walked in the door. I started talking to him, assuming all the while that he must be a famous basketball player or something. He asked me a lot of questions. I told him briefly what I had just been through and how I was getting my life together again and that I needed extra work. He grabbed a pen and paper and wrote down his address and phone number and told me to meet him the following morning.

He had a nice house, which I'd expected, but when he invited me inside, I couldn't help but notice that instead of basketball trophies on his shelf he had an Oscar. Next to that was an Emmy or a Tony (I can't remember which) and a few Golden Globes.

"You're an actor?" I asked, obviously confused.

"Yes, son. My name is Louis Gosset, Jr. and I'm an actor."

"Holy shit! You're the guy from *Officer and a Gentleman*?!"

"Yes, son. I was in that movie and a few others, too." And he smiled that great big movie star smile. I felt pretty stupid.

We walked back outside and he introduced me to his dogs, two massive black Labrador Retrievers named Kingfish and Tar Heel. I didn't know it yet, but those dogs were my angels. I was scared of them at first, even though they behaved pretty well in his presence. He showed me where the food was and where their leashes were and told me to come back every day to feed and walk them. He said he would give me $500 in advance for the next 30 days.

I couldn't believe it—I couldn't believe he was going to pay me so much money just to feed some dogs. He walked back inside to get his checkbook and the moment that door shut, the dogs jumped up and took me to the ground within two seconds. They overpowered me with no struggle at all. They had to have been 100 pounds each, if not heavier. They pinned me down and licked my face, ears, and hair. As soon as they heard the door opening, they obediently sat back down. I stood up and began wiping the slobber off of my face and neck as Mr. Gossett let out a loud laugh.

"I can see the dogs took a liking to you." And he handed me the check and went back inside.

When I got there the next morning, they heard me opening the gate and started whimpering and whining with excitement. As soon as that gate was open, they took me right to the ground again and began licking my face, happy just to see me. They didn't care if I had cologne on, designer jeans, even if I had brushed my teeth or not. We continued this routine daily. Most days it made me laugh, the way they behaved. A few times, though, I was so overwhelmed by their pure affection, I just curled up and cried. When that happened the dogs worked even harder to try to cheer me up, which made me cry even more.

When I first started the job, I was so out of shape I could only walk them to the end of the street and back. There was a seasonal creek bed that separated the road from a park and, when it rained, the creek ran heavy and formed a big pool. As soon as the water was in sight, Kingfish and Tar Heel broke into a full-out sprint and dove in. It was like a ride at the amusement park for them. Then they ran back, knocked me down, shook water all over me, and jumped into the pool again. They did this over and over and could not have been happier about it.

Sometimes they ran into the park and I'd have no choice

but to chase after them. Eventually my strength and endurance improved and instead of panting after them, I was running alongside them. Because of them I started swimming in the ocean. They had shown me that no matter what was going on, you could be happy just by jumping into the water. Such a simple, beautiful appreciation of life. And every time I opened that gate they taught me what it meant to love unconditionally, and boy did I need that love.

Mr. Gossett showed me the same kind of love. He didn't need me to walk his dogs. He had assistants and housekeepers. He gave me that job because he wanted me to earn an honest dollar and stay sober. That love brought me back to life and kept me going, day by day, just like the 12-step meetings.

As time went by, I became strong enough to hike with Kingfish and Tar Heel all through Zuma Canyon. I moved out of Baron's and into my sponsor Robbie's place. Instead of paying rent, he just had me wash his cars and dogs. I slept in an empty wing of his house—the place was so big, his wife didn't even know I was staying there.

A woman named Pietra hired me to take her young boys boogie boarding and she paid me $40 an hour to do it. I got a job at the Malibu Ranch Treatment Center working the night shift, mostly because I still looked too messed-up to be there during the day.

A typical 18-hour workday looked like this: get off the graveyard shift at the treatment center at 7 o'clock in the morning and go to Mr. Gossett's house to walk and feed the dogs. As soon as I was done I would head to the beach and take the kids boogie boarding. After a quick disco nap lying on the sand, I'd jump into the ocean, rinse off, and head over to Sherman's place to wash dogs, then head back over to Robbie's house to wash his car.

It was important for me to stay busy. Not only did that mean I was making money, but it kept my mind off of relapsing and did a decent job of holding the anxiety and depression at bay. That changed when I saved up enough money to move out of Robbie's house and rent a guesthouse. Once I was alone, my old neuroses started manifesting. After all the things I'd done and places I'd been, I had a lingering, creeping paranoia that I couldn't shake. I was convinced someone was coming to kill me. I would get up 15 times a night to make sure the door was locked. When I got up in the morning I'd take all the food out of the refrigerator and inspect it to make sure no one had poisoned it during the night.

I didn't tell anyone about my irrational fears, not even Robbie. I became obsessed with the notion that the FBI was coming after me because of the things I'd done, or some movie star was seeking vengeance because I'd dated and done drugs with his daughter.

Robbie bought me an inflatable mattress so I wouldn't have to sleep on the floor anymore, and one night I woke to the sound of rats scurrying all around me.

I turned on the light and there was nothing. Just an empty room.

I switched the lights off and lay back down. Then I heard them again, but this time louder. I had flashbacks of when I was homeless, sleeping in alleys, and rats would crawl over me. I would get so scared that I would just clench my eyes shut and pretend like it wasn't happening.

I jumped up and thrashed around, yelling and cursing. I

ran out of the house and called Robbie sobbing: "They're in the mattress! They're inside the mattress!"

He drove over much faster than I thought it would take him to get there. He jumped out of his car with a flashlight and went inside the guest house. He looked everywhere. After a few minutes he came outside and looked at me with a noticeably sad look on his face. It was a look of sympathy.

"There aren't any rats, Khalil."

"Yes there are!"

"Come here," Robbie said as he took me into the guest house. I was shaking. He deflated the mattress and rolled it up. "Do you see that? No rats."

"I can't take it anymore!" I yelled. "People are coming to get me. They're following me. They want to kill me!"

Robbie guided me into a chair and listened to me rant and rave for 10 or 15 minutes. I kept telling him that they were coming—the cops, the government, aliens, the lunatic A-list movie star whose daughter I'd dated. When I had finally talked myself out, in a very compassionate and gentle voice, Robbie said, "Listen, I've got to tell you something and I don't want you to get offended by what I'm going to say, but it's really important that you understand this."

I was still crying. I took a deep breath. "Okay, what?"

He said, "There's no one looking for you."

"How do you know?"

"Khalil, just listen to me. There's no one looking for you. There's no one coming to kill you. Nobody is following you around looking to end your life."

"And how do you know this?"

"Because you're not that important," he said. "I'm from the lower east side of Manhattan, man. I lived there during the '70s. I hung out with people who hurt other people. I knew hit men. I dealt drugs. If there were people who wanted to harm or kill you, they would have done it a long time ago. They wouldn't do it now that you're sober, highly visible, going to meetings twice a day, and have a bunch of friends. They would have killed you when you were a homeless nobody. Khalil, it's just not true. You just aren't that important."

Just like the revelation about how the women in my life had escaped, I felt a noticeable shift take place. The bubble of paranoia I had built around myself was depressurized by his words and by the mere act of telling him about my fears in the first place. But I still ended up moving back into Robbie's house. I just wasn't ready to be alone yet.

I threw myself back into the 18 hour days. There were two major tools that helped me get through those marathons. One was an amazing book called *Around the Year with Emmet Fox*. Emmet Fox was a tremendous and influential spiritual leader who died in 1951. *Around the Year with Emmet Fox* is a collection of 365 meditations—one for each day of the year—and every morning when I got out of the treatment center I would read that day's entry. Mornings were when my depression, anxiety, and feelings of impending doom were the most intense, so these daily affirmations were a welcome reprieve. It gave me something to focus on and think about while I worked during the day.

The other tool that helped me manage the hectic schedule was Tony Robbins' Hour of Power. A great friend of mine named Matthew had given me the CDs and they detailed the best way to start your day. The program included 30 to 60 minutes of breathing exercises, incantations, and a gratitude list, all of which was perfect for when I walked the dogs.

I started every day with Emmet Fox and the Hour of Power, and throughout the day I'd slip in exercise, meetings, meditation, and prayers whenever I could. It was incredible. It felt so good to lay that foundation and to finally feel some sort of strong spiritual connection to whatever it was that created me and this beautiful earth.

To top it all off, my mom called to tell me the cancer was gone. Her insurance had covered the treatment.

Thank God.

Two years into sobriety I had managed to save up about $14,000. I worked non-stop and was way too busy to ever spend my money. And $14,000 was a fortune for someone like me. I busted my ass every day to make that money and I cashed every check as soon as I got it, which was kind of a nightmare because I couldn't get a bank account and I certainly couldn't get a credit card, so I would have to drive to check cashing places deep in the Valley or in Santa Monica, which kicked up all kinds of old shit, including cravings.

I kept all of the cash in hundreds wrapped up in rubber bands hidden underneath my sink. Soon, instead of getting up and reading Emmet Fox or praying, I would pull the money out and count it and recount it every morning. I became obsessed with it. I started fantasizing about having more of it, lots more. I started thinking about all of the shit I was gonna buy and how good it would make me feel. Mostly I imagined what kind of car I was gonna get. At the time, I was driving a 1987 Volvo with well over 200,000 miles on it—it was basically an ashtray on wheels.

I became more and more consumed by the idea of making money and started thinking up all kinds of get-rich-quick schemes. Living in Malibu was bizarre because everybody around me was so rich, or at least their parents were. All my friends drove Escalades and Range Rovers, fully paid for by mom and dad. I loved them but I was so jealous of them at the same time. It ate me alive.

I was about to make some money, a lot of money, and quickly. Or so I thought.

* * *

Through the 12-step meetings I met a guy named Daniel. His parents and grandparents were incredibly wealthy and when his father died, Daniel inherited millions. He was super good-looking and charismatic, which was somewhat infuriating, but I liked him. When he got out of rehab, he asked me to sponsor him, so we spent a lot of time together. During our talks he told me he was investing in futures and options, buying contracts of silver and gold, and making a ton of money. He'd turned $40,000 into $800,000 in fewer than 90 days.

I was fascinated and eager to learn more, so I asked some other people about it. Every single one of them, without fail, said, "Don't invest in futures or options. Everybody loses money on that. Everybody."

Yeah, I thought, *except I'm gonna be different.*

Even Daniel didn't want me to do it. "It's a very volatile market, Khalil. You can lose a lot of money. Quickly."

In some deluded flash of paranoia, I began to suspect that Daniel just didn't want me to have any money, which filled me with rage and made me pester him about it even more. He finally agreed to let me come in on buying some of the silver and gold contracts.

I drove to Daniel's house and handed him the entire $14,000.

"I've got a good feeling," I said. "I'm going all in."

He must have said "no" 20 times but I eventually wore him out. He invested every penny into contracts of gold for me. Within a few days gold went up, just like I'd thought, and I made a bunch of money. I can't recall the exact figure, but it's certainly safe to say I caught "gold fever."

Daniel called me. "All right, Khalil, you've made some money. Are you ready to sell?"

"Look, man, I'm in it. Gold's gonna go parabolic. I'm in it for the long haul." I had no prior knowledge of the market and was throwing around words I barely even understood and yet there I was, calling shots like I was the Oracle of Omaha.

"Why don't you just pull back half your position?" Daniel suggested.

"No," I said. "I don't wanna pull back half my position. I wanna make some fucking money."

I stayed all-in and gold kept going up. There were a few hiccups, but the rebounds had me making more and more money. Watching the market on CNBC became my new addiction. I couldn't sleep. I quit reading and abandoned my prayers and meditation. I was short with people because they didn't understand the stress I was under from chasing the ups and downs of the market.

I continued to run with Kingfish and Tar Heel because I loved those dogs, but I started skipping the 12-step meetings and hanging around with a lot of different girls instead. Just being sober wasn't good enough anymore—now I needed to be rich.

After a few weeks, the market was looking very shaky and Daniel asked me again if I wanted to sell.

"No," I said firmly.

He tried everything he could think of to convince me otherwise, but I wouldn't budge. I was convinced that gold was finally going to make its one big push upwards. I got up around 3:00 a.m. the next morning to see where gold was at on the international market. Things were looking good. I went downstairs to wait for the US market to open. My sleep had been horrible for weeks and my exhaustion finally caught up with me—I passed out in a beanbag chair sometime around 6:00 a.m.

I woke up four and a half hours later. The television was on silent. I looked to the top of the screen to see where gold was at. My heart dropped. I rubbed my eyes hard and opened them back up, my vision still a little blurry. Gold had fallen massively—down over $32 an ounce. Still staring at the screen, I scrambled for my phone as I tried to do the math in my head. It was something like for every dollar gold had gone down, I would lose $1,000.

Why hadn't Daniel called me? He must have sold my position when it started to drop.

I looked down at my phone to dial his number and I realized it was off. The battery had died. I plugged it in and when it turned on, it showed seven voicemails, all of them from Daniel.

"Hey, buddy. Do you want to sell? Call me back."

"Khalil, it's Daniel. You need to sell now, man. Call me."

"Call me."

I didn't bother listening to the last four voicemails. I dialed Daniel's number. It felt like the room was tilting sideways. My forehead felt numb.

Daniel picked up on the first ring. My money was completely gone. All of those 18-hour days, working seven days a week, saving every penny...I crumbled. I fell on the ground and burst into tears as I punched myself in the leg and yelled, "No, no, no!"

I was so mad at Daniel for not selling even though I had explicitly told him not to sell. I was mad at myself. I was mad at God. "How could you do this to me, God? How could you do this to me? I've tried so hard, I've worked so hard. How could you do this to me?"

Daniel understood my rage but there was nothing he could do about it. He had lost a lot of money as well. He had to go back to Louisiana to visit his mother so he could pull more from his trust and he asked me if I could house-sit. So there I was, alone in his beautiful million-dollar home on Point Dume in Malibu, getting my nose rubbed in the fact that I would never have anything like it.

That night was miserable. I couldn't sleep. I kept thinking about all the money I'd lost. The next morning, I shuffled into Daniel's living room, a steady stream of tears rolling down my face. "God, how could you do this to me? I worked so fucking hard."

I fell onto the couch. *I can't do this anymore*, I thought. *I can't go on any more. I'm 35 years old and I'm fucking broke and I'm never gonna have a life.*

I lay there and dwelled on the fact that my life was half over and there I was, without a fucking penny, a high school dropout, convicted felon, and ex-junkie. I must've lain there for hours, submerged in that musty swamp of self-loathing and self-pity.

When I finally found the strength to lift myself up off the sofa, I looked over at the coffee table and sitting right in the middle of it was a brand-new copy of *Around the Year With Emmet Fox*. I had given it to Daniel the previous Christmas. I hadn't read my copy in months because I'd been so caught up in the market. I had lost my way yet again, not to the depth and darkness of being a homeless junkie, but at the time it felt pretty close. Seeing the book on the table only made me feel worse. Now I was completely broke *and* felt like a piece of shit for abandoning the amazing spiritual path I'd been on.

I picked it up and flipped through the pages to that day's date. What I saw next is still hard to believe, even a decade later. In fact, if I saw it in a movie I would think, *Oh, bullshit, man. Stuff like that never happens.* But stuff like this does happen. I know because it happened to me. When I looked at the top of the page for that day's date, the entry said:

"Do not put your faith in silver and gold. Put your faith in God."

Goosebumps ran over my entire body and time stood still.

God hadn't done anything to me. God had never told me to invest in futures. In fact, He had probably sent me a hundred messengers telling me not to.

There are no shortcuts. There is only the straight and narrow. My job is to work, be kind, and help people. To live an honest life to the best of my ability.

I knew I was 100% responsible for everything going on in my life, good and bad. Whatever I put in is what I was going to get out, and it was time to go all-in.

Not with silver and gold—with myself.

CHAPTER EIGHT

AFTER I LOST EVERYTHING IN THE GOLD AND SILVER MARKET,
I could not get back to the spiritual path fast enough. And
when I found it again, I clung to it like a drowning man seizes
a life preserver. I started going to the Self-Realization Fel-
lowship Lake Shrine Temple regularly and meditating there.
After my meditation, I would sit in silence by the lake and
watch the swans glide across the water, absorbing the energy
of all of that beauty.

On Sundays I went to the Hare Krishna Temple, which
was packed with the most amazing people chanting loudly,
crying out to the Lord. There was always an abundance
of amazing vegetarian food. You could eat as much as you
wanted and it was all free. They put so much effort into
preparing this food. They started it on Saturday morning,
and they'd chant and pray over it for 24 hours, infusing it
with their spiritual bliss before they served it. I ate myself
blind every Sunday afternoon and sometimes I even joined
in on their dancing. I jumped around with them and chanted:
"Hare Krishna Hare Krishna, Krishna Krishna Hare Hare,

Hare Rama Hara Rama, Rama Rama Hare Hare."

It was during this time that my friendship with one of the most amazing human beings I have ever met, Sean French, picked up seamlessly right where it had left off years earlier. Sean had tried desperately many times to get me to slow down with the drugs. Toward the end, he had done everything in his power to get me to stop. The last time I'd seen him, I'd been having one of my "episodes." I had been tearing my face apart in the mirror and pulling large clumps of hair out from my head with the scalp still attached. He had tried to barricade me into the bathroom and had called the police. I'd broken the door down and run away. When I called him and told him I was sober and wanted to hang out, I was scared he might hang up on me. Instead he asked me for my address and said, "I'll be right over."

He showed up an hour later with grocery bags full of stuff—exotic looking produce, herbs, supplements—most of which I'd never even heard of before. Stinging nettles, burdock, turmeric. He took all of that and more, put it in a blender, and told me to drink it down.

I took a sip. "It tastes like shit."

"I don't care. Drink it."

I did. And I felt amazing. I started drinking Sean's smoothies and juices every day and tweaking the recipes to make them more palatable—some honey and lemon with the turmeric, and apple cider vinegar and cayenne with the ginger—and it became much easier to ingest these concoctions that made me feel so profoundly different.

I was hooked. I started regularly driving an hour to the tonic bar at Erewhon in West Hollywood and would sit there for hours, inspired by the amazing energy and fresh, organic ingredients. I practically lived at the Vitamin Barn, a juice bar in Malibu, and I was delighted when they adopted the açaí bowl craze that was taking place in South America and Hawaii, made with the now famous purple superfruit from Brazil. Then I discovered Rawesome (a.k.a. "The Raw Garage") where I loaded up on raw milk, yogurt, and butter. Then came One Life, a natural food store in Venice. Then Rawvolution, a raw vegan restaurant on Main Street in Santa Monica. And so on and so on.

It wasn't long before I began fantasizing about opening up my own juice bar, where I could take my favorite elements from the health food shops I loved so much and combine them with the superfoods Sean had introduced me to, but make them tasty and palatable. Except I wanted my place to be 100% organic. And I wanted to hire clean, happy, healthy people from the local community instead of white kids with dreads and dirt under their nails who reeked of patchouli oil and were seeking an identity through drug use, reggae, and veganism. Something about the latter made most of those places feel like I was being punished for wanting to eat healthy.

Why couldn't there be a place like Starbucks for healthy, organic food? I wasn't even a great lover of coffee, but I was in love with what they did there. The stores were always clean, comfortable, well-lit, and felt safe, with great music playing. The staff was clean, happy, and helpful. I was enamored. I never had intentions of becoming a giant company like them, but I loved the idea of creating a community living room within walking distance of where I lived. A place where our neighbors could take their kids to get organic frozen yogurt after their Little League games instead of garbage full of high fructose corn syrup and chemicals. A place where people could go for organic juices, organic coffee—organic everything, really. A place for the community to come together, away from their cell phones, laptops, and "social networks."

I convinced Daniel to invest in the idea and even signed a lease at a run-down little shopping center near Zuma Beach, about a mile away from Robbie's place. Then Murphy's law kicked in: Daniel relapsed, the woman who was supposed to vacate the space exercised her option to stay, and the whole deal fell apart. I was heartbroken.

※　※　※

I got promoted to daytime shifts at the Malibu Ranch Rehab Center, which was quite a circus but it helped me to stay sober, watching these people come in all fucked-up with big court cases pending or husbands or wives who had just finally left them, as well as seeing people at a physical bottom, still reeling from the recent news that they had Hepatitis C or HIV.

One of the clients there, a young girl who was a complete mess, said she wanted to start going to yoga. I volunteered to go with her, mostly because she was really cute and I had no boundaries. Her parents were so grateful that she was going to start doing something healthy again that they gave me their credit card number to buy the two of us 20 classes to split.

The plan was she would meet me at the yoga studio the next day, after her hair appointment in Santa Monica. One of the other techs would drop her off and I would take her home. I got there early and stood outside the yoga studio smoking, which seems so funny to me now, but at the time seemed totally normal. A flawlessly beautiful 5'10" brunette woman walked past. She smiled at me and walked inside the yoga studio. I threw my cigarette down and followed. When I walked in, she was standing behind the front desk.

"Can I help you?" she asked.

"Yeah, I'm supposed to meet my friend here. She wants to do yoga."

The woman smiled again. "Great. My name's Lydia. I'm teaching today. Are you taking the class, too?"

"Yes," I said, a little too loud and enthusiastically.

"Do you have a mat?"

"No, I don't."

She loaned me a mat and showed me where to set it up. What she didn't tell me was that the class was Level 3, which was for people with a very advanced practice. I had no idea what I was doing. Fifteen minutes in my whole body was shaking. I was pouring sweat, stumbling my way from one pose to the next. I was two years sober, taking vitamins and drinking smoothies and juices multiple times a day, but I was still severely out of shape—might've had something to do with my habit of also drinking Coca-Cola with lunch and dinner, eating Doritos every day, and helping myself to the occasional Jack in the Box binge.

Lydia walked over and placed her hand on my back. She pressed me down into Child's Pose.

"Just stay," she said.

I stayed there for about 10 minutes, then rolled over on my back into Savasana, Corpse Pose. The class was an hour and 15 minutes and I spent about an hour of it on my back, fading in and out of consciousness. But the room was bursting with healing energy and I felt incredible.

The girl from rehab never showed up, but from that day on I went to every one of Lydia's classes I could. I drastically reduced my smoking habit—it just didn't feel right to poison my body like that and then walk into a yoga studio. I began to cut out the junk food and started researching superfoods like goji berries, raw cacao beans, and bee pollen.

It took me six or seven more classes, but I finally started to pick up the poses and gain some momentum. Lydia was always complimenting and encouraging me. She wasn't just a beautiful woman; she was a goddess.

A couple weeks in, I was on my back in Savasana and Lydia walked over and pressed her thumb into the center of my forehead. Then she crossed her hands, placed them on my sternum, and fanned them out. When she pushed down, I started crying and I had no idea why. Her touch was so powerful. I was embarrassed but she kept her hands there, healing me from the inside out. A lifetime of pain and pressure slowly began to release.

Yoga is such a fascinating and powerful tool. All of the pain and trauma I had suffered through as a child, or put myself through as an adult, were stored deep within my tissue, locked into the muscle fibers. Yoga was the master key to unlocking and releasing them all.

Once again, it was a cute girl and a beautiful woman that led me further down my spiritual path. Pretty shallow and pretentious, but I'm not too proud to admit that I learned how to swim in the shallow end before I could swim in the deep end.

* * *

One day soon after, I was taking a break from work to grab a bite at a local Mexican restaurant in Malibu. As I was standing in line, I noticed a familiar face out of the corner of my eye. It was Jennifer. When our eyes met, I felt like I couldn't breathe. From the looks of it, so did she. We managed to get out our awkward hellos.

Finally, she said, "I thought you were dead. For the first year after you disappeared, every time I heard sirens I freaked out. I always thought you were dead."

"Why did you leave me?" I blurted out.

She began crying. "I didn't. They gave me pills and took me away. They hired someone to watch me 24 hours a day. They wouldn't let me use the phone. My grandfather hired private security to stay at the rehab to keep you away from me and to keep me from running back to you."

"I don't understand. Why did you leave me? You said you would never leave me..."

We went back and forth a few times like this. I must've asked Jennifer 10 times why she left me, not really hearing her response.

Finally I changed the topic. "Are you seeing anyone?"

She said she was. He was a television actor, a very handsome guy. I'll admit, it stung.

After that, our relationship was rocky with many ups and downs. There were periods of arguing and giving one another the silent treatment, followed by reconciliation, hugging, smiling, and laughing. But eventually we built a friendship. We had survived something together that no one else could understand, and some may not even believe.

She wanted to know *everything* that had happened to me. So I told her.

And that was that. Jennifer and I are great friends to this day.

* * *

Fred Segal is an amazing and accomplished man and an icon in the fashion industry. He pioneered the idea of jeans being a fashion statement and started his own boutique in Los Angeles, which spread to locations all over the world. Another one of his projects was a super high-end treatment center called The Canyon, located on a 300-acre property that he owns in Malibu, where the Dalai Lama would come stay from time to time. I had visited The Canyon once before because on Tuesday nights they held meetings and invited other treatment centers to attend. I fantasized about working in a place like that.

One day I was sitting outside The Coffee Bean in Malibu and I saw Fred Segal sitting at a table, talking with some friends. A strong urge overtook me and before I allowed my brain to talk me out of it, I walked right over, stood up straight, and loudly proclaimed, "Mr. Segal, I would do anything to work at your treatment center."

"It's Freddy," he replied.

"Okay, Freddy. I would do anything to work at your treatment center."

"Really?"

"Yeah."

"Do you have a pen?"

"No, sir."

"Well, go get a pen!" he barked.

I ran inside The Coffee Bean. I didn't even ask to borrow a

pen, I just grabbed one off the counter and ran back outside.

Freddy said "Write this down" and rattled off a phone number. "What's your name?"

"Khalil."

"Okay, Khalil. Call that number and ask for Leo and tell him Freddy said to hire you." And then he turned away and returned to his conversation, dismissing me without dismissing me. Poor Leo. I had no professional experience, education, or qualifications to work there. The Malibu Ranch certainly got my foot in the door but it was a free-for-all—everyone was sleeping together and the staff knew the clients were doing drugs and didn't care. But Leo hired me for overnight shifts and to fill in for day shifts when people called in sick. They didn't have a choice—Freddy owned the place.

I had no idea how to conduct myself in a professional manner. I got written up at least once a month. I just didn't know what the proper boundaries were for staff and clients and would say whatever I felt needed saying. Lucky for me, the people who ran the place were incredibly patient and came from a wide variety of backgrounds. And in hindsight, I think they did more work on me than they did on the clients—it took the whole village to raise this idiot.

Cathleen had a wall full of qualifications, master's and doctorates, and she was very loving and kind with me. Her focus was the professional application of mental health and social work, whatever the fuck that means.

Leo ran the joint and was really into Toltec Wisdom and *The Four Agreements* by Don Miguel Ruiz. Leo was friends with Mr. Ruiz and traveled extensively with him all over Mexico.

Kelly was an ex-attorney who had a passion for helping

children and did foster care for kids with special needs before he got into treatment. He spent endless hours with me working through cognitive behavioral therapy and dialectic behavioral therapy—to this day some of the greatest treatments I've ever received. The guy is a Samurai—one of the best there is.

Clients paid $60,000 a month to stay at The Canyon. I was getting paid 14 bucks an hour to work there, but I would have done it for free. I got just as much value, if not more, out of being there than many of the clients did, I guess because I wanted it. I really wanted help. I'd been sober for two and a half years and wanted to keep moving forward. I'm sure it would've been different if my parents had stuck me there or if I had something else to fall back on, like so many of the clients I saw come in and out, but I was desperate. Cathleen, Leo, and Kelly could see that I wanted to get well and become a better person, and they busted their asses to help me do it. To this day, I thank God they saw the potential in me, raw and unpolished as it may have been.

What I lacked in education I more than made up for with hustle. Even though I was on night shifts and fill-ins, I told every single person who worked there, "Please, if you ever want a day off, I would love to take your shift."

With a couple dozen people working there I soon had fill-in shifts every day, then it went to double and triple shifts. I loved it. I was making money and they even gave me medical and dental insurance, which I hadn't had since I was a kid. My life was starting to look and feel really incredible. I even formed a little crush on a girl who worked at the Vitamin Barn, the juice bar in Malibu. Her name was Hayley. She had the most amazing smile and gorgeous big blue eyes. I found myself going in three times a day, hoping she would be there so we could have our routine 5- to 10-minute conversation while I sipped my smoothie at the bar. I was too nervous to ask her out but couldn't shake the feeling that I knew her from somewhere.

I finally couldn't take it anymore and found the courage to ask her, "Why do I feel like I know you?"

"I don't know," she said. "I feel the same way. Maybe you know my sister."

"Who's your sister?"

"Eden."

I just about fainted.

"Oh my God," I finally said, stunned. "You're the little girl who shut the door in my face."

She smiled.

"Yeah, maybe."

And she walked away. I wasn't going to let the door close this time. From that day on I tried to be clever by mentioning upcoming concerts and movies, hoping the conversation would lead to us hanging out together. I'd order my smoothie and then say, "Oh, there's a really cool band playing at this place on Saturday." Then I'd wait for her to ask me about it.

She never did. I got nothing from her.

The next day: "Hey, have you heard about this movie? It's supposed to be great."

She'd just smile and walk away.

I started buying the LA Weekly and studying it, scouring for anything that might appeal to her and get a response. Music, foreign films, art galleries—nothing worked. It drove me nuts. But I was infatuated with her. I wasn't going to give up.

* * *

While Hayley was driving me crazy by ignoring me, my job at The Canyon was getting even better. The other owner of the treatment center was a man named Michael Cartwright, who rose from the depths of despair and addiction to become incredibly successful in the mental health and treatment industry. He regularly visited from his home in Nashville and he began to take notice of my passion and work ethic.

During one visit he took me out to dinner and said, "Khalil, you're what I call a producer. You produce results. You're a worker and you're a producer. I want to help you educate yourself. What do you want to do?"

I was incredibly flattered. I had never thought of myself in that light. Junkie? Sure. Unlovable? Probably. But a producer? That was a new one.

"I'd love to do interventions. I could help people get the treatment they need and I could make a bunch of money, too."

He wasn't fazed by the last part of my response.

"Okay," he said. "We can get you training to become an interventionist. Now let's figure out where you want to be in one year, three years, and five years."

I started to tell him and he held up a hand.

"No, write it down and show me."

I started explaining again and again he said, "No. Write it down. It's very, very important. You'll understand some day."

He was right. There is a definite power in taking pen to paper and coming up with a concrete plan. Michael arranged for me to take a course to become a certified interventionist and he paid for it in full. He also sent me to conferences for continuing education and networking and encouraged the other staff at The Canyon to help me continue to grow.

Now I had some credentials to my name and I began doing interventions and, much to my delight, making money. I still had no clue how to act like what was considered "a professional," which is probably why I was so successful at what I did. Most drug addicts are incredibly smart and quite suspicious. Over the years, they learn to not trust doctors or psychiatrists and to despise authority figures. I am an outlaw, a rebel—always have been, always will be. I say inappropriate shit and will go out of my way to make somebody laugh. These people were in pain, massive amounts of pain, just like I was. I didn't care that we weren't supposed to become friends with clients—a friend was exactly what they needed.

Imagine being one of the only survivors in a horrible plane crash—the trauma, the fear, the guilt, and the nightmares. You could go see five psychologists or psychiatrists or so called "specialists"—and I'm not saying that you couldn't get some value out of it—but then imagine you meet someone who had also been one of the only survivors of a horrible plane crash, but it had happened years ago and they were now in recovery and fully functioning. You would listen to that person, that plane crash survivor, and they could help you because they've been where you've been and could speak the absolute truth from experience.

I have respect for therapists and psychiatrists, I suppose, but if you're a fucking drug addict and you're in pain and you're scared and you don't think you can stop, well guess what? I'm a fucking drug addict, too, and I stopped. And there's priceless value in the therapeutic process of the two of us sitting together and shooting the shit.

When I looked those clients in the eye, with them knowing everything I'd done and been through, when I showed them unconditional love and told them, "You know what? You're gonna be okay," it gave them hope.

Nearly every single person I worked with one-on-one during my time at The Canyon is sober today. I'm still in contact with almost all of them. Through the grace of God and their willingness to put in the work, they made it. In fact, several of them are my best friends today.

By this point, I'd been working at The Canyon for over two years and was finally starting to get comfortable with sober life. I was reading a ton of self-help books, starting with *The Secret, Psycho-Cybernetics, The Power of Positive Thinking,* and *Think and Grow Rich.* My outlook on life and my self-esteem really began to improve and my paranoia had, for the most part, completely disappeared. All of this was spearheaded by a conversation Robbie and I had late one night after a 12-step meeting. I launched into one of my typical diatribes about how sad my childhood was and how I was molested and how bad my parents were. Robbie raised his voice with me.

"That was three decades ago," he said. "Do you really think there's any value in you telling those stories over and over again?"

He looked at me, glassy eyed as if he was about to cry. He gave me a look that I suppose a loving father would give his son. And then he hit me with another one of his life-altering questions.

"Who would you be without your story?"

"What are you talking about?" I asked.

"Who would you be? Who would you be if you stopped telling the same sad fucking story over and over again of what happened to you? If you just dropped all of it, stopped talking about drugs all the time and what you did when you were on them. Stopped talking about all of the shit that happened to you when you were a kid. You're 37 years old now. No one's trying to hurt you. No one's coming after you. No one's going to hold you down and molest you. You haven't done drugs in three years. Stop fucking talking about them. Stop glamorizing them. Who would you be without your story? Who would you become?"

He turned around and walked upstairs to bed.

I sat there in shock, chain-smoking my Camel Lights. My body was paralyzed. My whole life I had been telling myself the same story—the world was bad, I was bad, God had forsaken me—and I believed it. I believed it with just as much conviction as I believed the sky was blue. God hadn't forsaken me, I had forsaken myself. My mother hadn't abandoned me—she had done the best she could with the tools she'd had.

I read somewhere that 90% of the thoughts we have every day are repetitions of the same thoughts we had the day before, and the day before that, and so on. We tell ourselves the same shit over and over each day and we wonder why we never change. Our thoughts stay the same, our habits stay the same, so our lives stay the same. I could read every self-help book ever written, but it wouldn't matter if I continued to cling to my story like a life preserver.

* * *

I'd been very careful with my money while working at The Canyon. I never invested in futures again, but I was incredibly paranoid about the economy and terrified of being broke and homeless again, so every other Friday I took my paycheck to Bank of America, cashed it, then drove straight to California Numismatic Metals in Inglewood and bought gold bullion. After my expenses were handled, every cent of every paycheck, bonus check, and everything I earned from private consultations and interventions went into pre-1933 Saint-Gauden MS64 gold coins, which I stashed in a safety deposit box. I started buying gold at around $500 an ounce and continued to buy as I watched the price steadily continue to rise. Within three years the coins I'd purchased for around $600 apiece were each worth $2,400.

I had a vision board propped up on the dresser in my bedroom with images that represented success to me. Pasted on it was a picture of a brand new Volvo XC90. Years earlier, I had found myself in the back seat of one and although it might sound silly—I know most guys would fantasize about a Porsche or a Ferrari or something—there was something special about the XC90. It felt so safe. I made a promise to myself that one day I would have my own.

In a rare show of excess, I decided to make one of my visualizations a reality. One of the girls I did an intervention on worked in the finance department at a Volvo dealership in Pasadena and, when I told her about my dream car, she said she could help me get it. I told her that I had destroyed my credit (I had simply stopped paying all my bills and credit cards around the time I'd started dealing ecstasy) and my score was only 460.

"I told you," she said. "I work in the finance department. I'll get it handled."

A week later I drove off the lot in a brand new silver 2006 Volvo XC90. It was mine, and it was beautiful.

So I was sober, reading great books, and had a bunch of

gold bullion in a safety deposit box and a car I was proud to drive, but the one thing I hadn't acquired yet was even a tiny amount of humility. I drove my coworkers at The Canyon crazy. They would tell me again and again, "Khalil, at the end of your shift you have to do your paperwork. You have to fill out these forms, these charts, and blah blah blah."

I never did. Just like I never did homework in school—and I mean *never*—I simply ignored the rules when it came to something I didn't want to do. I should have been shown the door dozens of times, but because I was a great producer of results and income they tolerated me. Eventually, though, my behavior and attitude overwhelmed my contributions. I got fired.

I was devastated. I resented them for firing me, but deep down I knew I was just not employable. If I could have kept my mouth shut and done the work I was supposed to do, I would have kept the job. Ideally it would have been enough to simply care for the clients and truly, passionately, and authentically believe in and love them. That's what kept them sober, not paperwork. That's what I felt—what I *knew*— and that's what got me fired.

Fear and depression immediately rose up like a tidal wave. I was 37 years old with a very limited set of professional experience, a new car payment, and the girl of my dreams had finally started to acknowledge me. The thought of going back to cleaning houses and washing dogs for lunch money was terrifying. I would do it, but I wanted to do more. I wanted to help people.

I tried to focus on all the positives: I had gotten a lot of people into treatment and helped many of them on their path to recovery. And even though I was terribly panicked about losing everything I'd saved, I kept telling myself not to dwell on money.

"Do not put your faith in silver and gold. Put your faith in God."

I didn't know when my next paycheck was going to come. But I didn't have to know—I just had to stay sober, stay positive, and do the footwork. The rest would take care of itself.

With that mindset, I left The Canyon for the last time and went to the Vitamin Barn to get some sustenance in me, but mostly so I could see Hayley, who always made me feel amazing just by looking at me.

She wasn't there that day. I sat there, hoping she would come in just so I could see her face. I had nowhere to go and no idea what to do with myself. The depression and anxiety crept closer. Then my phone rang. It was the parents of a girl I had helped get into rehab a couple years earlier.

"We need your help," the father said. "We have a tracking device inside our daughter's Blackberry. She's somewhere in Long Beach—we have an address but we don't know what it is, what kind of place it is. We're worried it might be dangerous."

I told them that Long Beach was pretty sketchy, but that I might be able to help.

"We don't care how much it costs," he said. "Please help our daughter."

They were talking about an extraction, pulling an addict out of a dangerous situation to get them the help they need, similar to what Jennifer's parents had done when they had taken her out of Spencer Recovery Center to keep her away from me. I gave the girl's father a list of people and places he could call.

"Look," he said, "there's no one we can call. There's no one else she would listen to. Can you please help us?"

"Of course."

I couldn't believe that an hour and a half after getting fired, I had my next job. I jumped in my car and I punched it, heading down PCH toward Long Beach. Toward the darkness.

CHAPTER NINE

THE ADDRESS WAS A CHEAP MOTEL. NOT QUITE A CRACK motel but maybe one step above.

I went to the front desk and gave them the girl's name. "I need to find her. Is she a registered guest here?"

"Yes, she is," the attendant said.

"Okay, I need you to take me to her room."

"Oh, we can't do that," he replied.

"Look, you can take me to her room or I'm going to have about 20 cops here in the next 3 minutes."

"Let me get somebody to watch the front desk."

He showed me to her room and I pounded on the door. When she opened the door, her jaw dropped.

"Oh my God, how did you find me? What are doing here? Get the fuck out of here!"

I was already in the room. Drugs and paraphernalia were scattered everywhere. There was a dangerous-looking, possibly homeless man sitting on the bed.

I told him, "Get your shit and get the fuck out of here right now or you're going to jail."

He disappeared out the door. I got the girl into my car and drove her to a sober living facility in Malibu. Her parents were overjoyed. Her dad handed me a check for $5,000 and my jaw almost dropped. I told them it was too much, but they wouldn't hear it. They had been spending that much every time they'd hired someone to do an intervention on her, which was about 15 times by then. A parent's worst nightmare is losing their kid. They had their daughter back, and that was priceless.

Soon after that I got a call from a father, a successful business owner, whose son was in trouble. He'd been resistant to treatment for a decade and the father thought he was finally going to lose his boy forever. I found the kid and got him to enter treatment. The father was so happy he not only wanted to pay me, he insisted on mentoring me and helping me network.

This became a pattern. I met a lot of very powerful, influential people because their kids were in trouble—it didn't matter if the kid was 16 or 45—and when I helped them, they spread the word throughout their circles. I handled extractions in some very tense situations, even going out of state to pull people out of meth labs. Whenever I knew things were going to be extremely dangerous, I'd call Scary Gary. Scary Gary was covered from head to toe in tattoos and had served more than half his life in prison. He was a terrifying man with a heart of pure gold. We'd met at a 12-step meeting, and when he'd found out what I did he'd said, "Let me know if you ever need backup." Scary Gary saved my ass on more than one occasion.

All the while, I fantasized about opening my own sober living. Instead of running around chasing people and putting myself in potentially life-threatening situations, *they* could come to *me* and I could take care of them and give them a beautiful, safe, healing place to live while they fought their demons. And not just 1 of them, 5 of them, maybe even 10. It was a dream that kept me going during some very dark times, one in particular.

It started with a call from a wealthy father who lived back east. I knew his daughter from The Canyon. She had been in and out of treatment for five years. Now she was living on the streets of Venice doing horrible things in order to survive. When girls like her disappear in Venice, it's typically in a place called Ghost Town. I was, unfortunately, intimately familiar with the area. Ghost Town was the last place I'd gotten high before my final overdose. That night I'd gotten jumped by a couple of knife-wielding crack dealers on the corner of Fourth and Brooks. I wasn't particularly looking forward to going back.

I had one lead on the girl: she was communicating with an ex-boyfriend from a Kinko's in the area. I staked the place out and cruised the rest of Ghost Town looking for her. Her parents called me non-stop, terrified she was going to die before I found her. It took me two weeks. When I walked up to her, she remembered me.

"Do you want to go get high?" I asked.

She was in full junkie paranoia mode, very suspicious of me. "Fuck you."

"No, I'm serious. Do you want to get high?"

"You relapsed?"

"Look, do you want to get high or not?"

"Do you have stuff on you?" she asked.

Fuck, she called my bluff. "I've got to go get it."

"Go get it and then I'll come with you," she said.

"Alright. Meet me back here in an hour." I drove away and called a friend who I knew was still using. "Hey, man, I need to score some black."

"Awesome!"

"No, not for me."

"No, it's cool," he said. "I won't tell anybody."

"Seriously dude, I'm three years sober. I'm not going to fuck this up. I just need to get some heroin."

"Hey, man, no judgment. Whatever."

He gave me his heroin dealer's number. We met up and I bought a gram. Then I went to a pharmacy on Santa Monica Boulevard where I used to talk the pharmacist into selling me boxes of needles, and when I left I had everything I needed to prove that I wanted to get high. I went back to meet the girl, but she wasn't there. I waited for 20 minutes, just me and the heroin and the box of needles. It was a pretty eerie feeling but getting high was the last thing on my mind.

When the girl finally resurfaced, she was barefoot, filthy, and clearly had been smoking crack. She got in the car and wanted to get high right away.

"Not in my car," I said. "We'll go somewhere where there's a bathroom."

We went to The Coffee Bean on Main Street because I knew they had a single stall, locking bathroom. I'm not saying I'm proud of this, but I can still, to this day, rattle off 20 safe bathrooms within 5 miles of that area that were perfect to shoot dope in. I gave her the heroin and she disappeared into the bathroom. I knew there was no way I could get her out of Venice unless she was high. She was too much of a flight risk and I didn't want to lose her.

I called her father. "I've got her. What do we do now?"

He wanted me to get her out of the country before she could run away and wind up back on the streets. Not to mention, they were part of a heavily connected political family in Chicago and he was scared that their names were going to get in the papers again. It had already happened when one of their sons had thrown a giant party and some really bad shit had gone down. The next story would be about their daughter prostituting herself for crack cocaine.

"Just get her out of there," he said. "I don't know, maybe take her down to Panama. Her ex-boyfriend's down there, the one she's been emailing."

I didn't have the time or patience to discuss it. "Great! Book the fucking tickets. Let's go right now."

"Okay. I'll call you back."

Twenty minutes went by, then 30. The girl was still locked in the bathroom. People were getting pissed, pounding on the door for her to come out. I could hear her muttering through the door so I knew she hadn't overdosed.

Eventually the girl behind the counter said, "Your friend needs to come out now."

"I'm really sorry, she's sick." I pounded on the door. "Let's go. Now."

She finally opened the door with blood smeared over both of her arms, dripping down to the floor. I dragged her to the parking lot and threw her in the car.

When I looked over at the passenger seat, she was trying to shove a needle into her arm.

"I'm sorry, I'm sorry," she said.

It was obvious she had no idea how to properly shoot up and I knew she wouldn't get on the plane any other way—the crack had made her too paranoid. I grabbed the needle, stuck it in her vein, pulled the plunger back to register the blood, then pushed off. I didn't even check to see how much she'd cooked up. Her entire body immediately went limp.

Oh shit. I just fucking killed this girl.

I slapped her a couple of times and she muttered a few words I couldn't quite understand. I raced to the AM/PM on Pico and Fourth Street and grabbed three Red Bulls. I pried her mouth open and started pouring them down her throat. She started to come to.

Phew. That was a close one.

Then my phone rang. It was her dad.

"There aren't any flights until midnight tonight."

"You've got to be kidding me." I looked over at this disaster of a person sitting in my car, covered in blood and vomit and Red Bull, nodding in and out of consciousness. Because I'd been looking for her I hadn't slept in a day and a half and couldn't remember the last time I'd eaten. I didn't want to admit it to myself, but smelling the cooked heroin and shooting her up had really shaken me. Add to that the fact that I'd almost killed her with an overdose, and I was reaching my limit. What the hell was I going to do with her until midnight?

We drove around for hours and stopped at the sober living where she had been staying, before she disappeared into Ghost Town, to pick up her suitcase and clothes. When I couldn't stand being in the car with her a moment longer, I got a hotel room near LAX. It was the last room available and the guy at the front desk told me it would be $450 for one night.

"Are you kidding me?" I said. "Can you just rent it to me for the evening?"

His eyes drifted to the girl, then back to me. "Sorry man, we don't do that here."

"No, no, no, that's not what I need it for."

"Yeah, right."

"All right. Just give me the fucking room." As soon as we got in I called room service. I was starving. "Please give me a Caesar salad. Give me your best steak, medium rare. And some French fries!"

The girl was nodding out on the bed but managed to mumble, "I'm hungry, too!"

"Okay, make me two of everything," I said into the phone. Then on a whim I asked, "Do you have any glass bottle Coca-Cola?"

"Yes."

"Wait, you have *glass* bottle Coca-Cola?"

"Yes, sir, we do."

More proof that God exists. I loved glass bottle Coca-Cola because it was made with real cane sugar and it reminded me of being a kid.

"Two of those, please!"

I hung up and walked over to the girl, who was muttering some incoherencies and drooling. I managed to figure out that she was asking me what we were doing.

"Just hanging out," I said. "Everything's cool."

By the time the food showed up, my mood had shifted. I was so happy to have finally found the girl and knew that I was about to eat a great steak and to top it off, drink a glass bottle Coca-Cola afterwards. I gave that waiter the best tip of his life. He took the lids off the plates and left the room. I sat down, my mouth watering. Before I could take a bite the girl started crying. She couldn't figure out her fork and knife. I got up and cut a few bites of steak for her, made sure she could get it into her mouth, then sat down again to enjoy my feast.

I had the first bite halfway to my mouth when I heard the sound of retching. I looked up and she was vomiting everywhere. I screamed at her and ran into the bathroom to grab a towel. I tried to hold it over her face to catch the puke without getting any of it on me. No dice. She vomited all over my hands and arms, a vile mixture of Red Bull and undigested steak. I couldn't take it anymore. I cussed her out something awful. Then I thought about all the times I'd been the one puking and shitting everywhere and figured this was karmic payback and actually started to laugh a little.

I wrangled her into the tub and got the shower going. When she was as close to clean as I could get her, she went back to the bed.

"I need to smoke," she said.

I knew she meant heroin, and at that point I didn't care. I had to get her on a plane and out of the country without her knowing what was going on, and her being high would hopefully make it easier. When the time came we took a taxi to LAX—I left my car at that hotel for 39 days. By the time we got to security I had to physically hold her up. A TSA agent stopped us.

"What's going on here?"

"I'm so sorry," I said. "My friend is terrified of flying. She just took a bunch of Xanax."

"Does she have a prescription for that Xanax?" another agent chimed in.

I looked him dead in the eyes and said, "Of course."

"Go ahead," he said as he waved us through.

This girl was higher than a fucking kite and had fresh track marks up and down her arm, but it was late; they were probably exhausted. We made it onto the plane and she stayed passed out for the entire six-hour flight to Panama. I didn't dare close my eyes, terrified that she would die in her sleep.

When we landed I nearly had to carry her off the plane. Her ex-boyfriend picked us up and drove us to Panama City to an old neighborhood called El Cangrejo. He had rented a tiny apartment on the 17th floor of a building that had steel cages on all the doors and windows.

When the door was locked behind us, I finally relaxed and handed her off to the ex-boyfriend.

"Buddy, I haven't slept in fucking days," I said. "I'm starving. I've got to take a shower. I've got to brush my teeth. It tastes like someone died in my mouth. I've got heroin, blood, puke, and sweat all over me."

"No problem," he said.

He showed me to the back bedroom, the only room with air conditioning. I took the longest shower of my life, cranked up the AC, and passed out. When I woke up the girl was still sleeping. The ex-boyfriend and his brother were keeping watch on her.

I took her purse and her passport and handed them to the brother.

"Do me a favor and go to the nearest FedEx and ship this overnight to her parents."

With that done, it would be impossible for her to escape and make it back to the States. She finally woke up a couple of hours later. She looked at her ex-boyfriend, then looked at me, back and forth a few times, trying to figure out what was happening.

She finally asked me, "What the fuck? Where are we?"

"We're in Panama," I said.

She snapped to full alert. "Where's my stuff? Where's my purse? Where's my passport?"

"Right now, probably half way back to your parents' house."

She leaped up and attacked me. The ex-boyfriend and I had to fight her off until she lost steam, then we pinned her to the ground until she stopped struggling. When we were certain she was done fighting, I walked him away to discuss what we were going to do next.

From across the room she sat up, looked at me, and very calmly said, "When you go to sleep, I'm going to kill you."

We removed every sharp object from the apartment. Every pen, knife, and fork, even the spoons. It took about two weeks for her to stop going through acute withdrawal. She didn't speak to any of us the whole time, other than a few incidences of her dangling on the window ledge, threatening to jump if we didn't let her go back to the States. When she finally did start talking it went something like this: "I want to go home. Fuck you. I hate you. I wanna get high. I fucking hate you."

Most of the time I kept my cool, but on more than one occasion I tackled her, took her to the ground, and held her in a chokehold until she went limp and twice I hit her, but only in self-defense. She may have been a junkie, but she was an ex-gymnast and stronger than a lot of the guys I had fought.

I ended up staying in that apartment for 38 days, and every night I slept with one eye open. For the next several months after that, I flew back and forth to Panama every week to check on her. Each time I visited, she was better than the time before, until eventually she was like a whole new person—a beautiful, thriving young woman.

We're great friends to this day and I'm happy to say she no longer wants to kill me.

* * *

Whenever I was in Malibu and not too busy babysitting drug addicts, I would go to the Vitamin Barn. Eating healthy was a huge part of my recovery, but I mostly went because I wanted to see Hayley. One day I was sitting in there babbling to her about some movie I wanted to go see.

She said, "Look, if you want my number, you have to ask me for it."

I froze. "Oh, sure. Can I get your number?"

She wrote it down and handed it to me.

It's been well established that I can be a complete idiot, and I didn't miss this opportunity to prove it.

"You should put your name on it because lots of girls give me their number."

A random stranger who overheard me slapped his hand over his face and shook his head. Hayley just walked away. I waited the mandatory three days to call her. I felt like I was going to throw up when I finally dialed her number. I asked her if she wanted to go see this movie that had just come out called *The Science of Sleep*.

"Yeah, sure. When?"

Oh my God. Oh my God. How can she be so nonchalant?

I picked her up and we went for sushi at a place called Kushiyu.

When the food came I could barely eat. Hayley ate more than any girl I'd ever met. I was shocked how she just kept eating and eating. Most girls would be embarrassed to eat that much. Shit, most *guys* would be embarrassed to eat that much. I was thoroughly impressed. We went to the movie, which told the story of a guy who was in love with a girl but was afraid to tell her, and she felt the same way about him. It was incredible. A must-see for anyone who hasn't seen it. And talk about hitting one out of the ballpark for a first date movie. Sometimes the universe just works with you.

I drove her home that night and couldn't think straight the entire time. Before our date I'd spent hours putting a CD together with just the right songs so when we drove we'd have the perfect soundtrack, all the while imagining us riding along, holding hands, enjoying the music in pure bliss. When I hit "play," I couldn't contain myself. I started belting out all the lyrics and stomping my foot as I drove, pounding on the steering wheel and singing at the top of my lungs. Basically making a complete fool of myself.

Hayley did not seem fazed by any of it. When we got to her place I didn't try to hug or kiss her. I just said good-night. We went out on dates almost every night for the next few weeks, and every night ended the same. I would tell her goodnight and drive away. I was so madly, wildly in love with her and was convinced she would never want to be with me. There was a significant age gap between us (18 years to be exact), but even without that she was way out of my league. I didn't care. I was satisfied with the friendship, but I still dreamed about the two of us holding hands and taking walks, holding hands and driving—holding hands and doing anything, really.

When I was working at the Canyon, I helped an NHL player get sober, prior to him going to the Olympics. He was in town and invited me to come see him play, so of course I asked Hayley to go with me. During halftime, or whatever they call it in hockey, we went up to grab a bite to eat and she leaned into me and rested her head against my shoulder. I couldn't breathe. I nervously ate a couple French fries as I quickly and forcefully pushed aside my fear of rejection, then I leaned in and kissed her. And she kissed me back.

After the game we went to a party at the Standard Hotel in downtown LA. We were on the roof, looking out over the skyline. I was nervously babbling about God knows what, when she turned toward me and kissed me. We kissed for hours on that rooftop.

CHAPTER TEN

I WAS STILL SECRETLY STAYING IN THE EMPTY WING OF ROB-
bie's house, which isn't a great situation when you have a
steady girlfriend. I would sneak into the house after 11 o'clock
at night and I'd be out by 7:00 a.m. the next morning to make
sure Robbie's wife Lori never saw me. The two of them had
enough problems with each other—Lori even slept in the
guest house—and the last thing I wanted to do was cause
more trouble for Robbie.

Then one morning I overslept. My room was upstairs and
all of the windows were open. Lori's guesthouse was right
below my room and all her windows were open, too. I saw
her leaning on one of the windowsills making a call. My cell
phone rang—a long, echoing ring.

Fuck, fuck, fuck.

I thought she'd seen me. I ducked down below the
window and answered.

Lori always spoke loudly, and I could hear her voice
coming from the guest house better than through the phone.
She hollered that she was going to New York and Europe

223

with Robbie, and she wanted somebody responsible to stay at the house and keep an eye on things.

"Can you do that?" she said.

I kept my voice very low and muffled. "Yes, sure."

She sensed something was wrong. "Is that too much to ask? You don't have to say yes. I'll pay you."

"No, no, no," I mumbled. It was too surreal. She was offering to pay me to do what I'd been doing for almost a year without her knowing about it. I housesat for them while they were away and when they came back, I just never left. I stayed there for a total of a year and a half, spanning my time at The Canyon, doing interventions and extractions, and falling madly in love with Hayley, until Robbie and Lori started fighting about selling the house. She wanted to sell, he wanted to stay, and they argued about it non-stop.

I was certain I'd need to find a new place to live, which was terrible. I'd never again be able to live rent-free on such an amazing Malibu estate. It was a 7,000-square-foot house with a private beach, two guest houses, and a saltwater swimming pool. As Robbie and Lori were yelling at each other one day, I had a vision, a moment of inspiration, or as they like to say in 12-step programs, a God-shot.

I discreetly interjected. "I'll rent the house from you."

That stopped the argument, at least for a moment.

"How are you going to afford it?" Lori asked.

"I'll pay you $10,000 a month."

Fair market value would have been closer to $15,000, maybe $20,000.

"How are you going to do that?" Lori asked.

"I can do it. I can sell all my gold. It's gone way up in value. I have more than enough. If you can give me a couple of months free on the front end, I'll fix the place up, I'll paint it, I'll make it beautiful. I want to turn this house into the best sober living in Malibu."

I knew it was an incredible long shot. I held my breath as I waited for her to answer.

"Okay. Just make sure you don't mess up my house."

"I won't. I'll take good care of it."

I almost fainted as I walked upstairs to begin planning the opening of my very own sober living, called Riviera Recovery.

* * *

Before I could even get the place painted and fixed up, clients started moving in. By then I had made a ton of connections in the treatment community and they knew I specialized in difficult cases. I never accepted the idea that anyone was too far gone to save, provided they *wanted* the help. And if they did, then I was willing to love them unconditionally and do everything in my power to show them that life could be fun, exciting, and meaningful without drugs or alcohol.

My methods were incredibly unorthodox. I took the clients to rock concerts, Vegas, health spas, Coachella, and Hawaii. One year, a bunch of us even went to the Bahamas and stayed on a yacht for a month, sailing from island to island.

I broke a lot of rules. All of them, probably. Many people criticized me and my methods, but I didn't care. They worked. And a lot of people got better.

I took clients paddleboarding most days and dragged them to yoga the others. We would fast and do three-week cleanses with fresh juices, raw foods, and colonics. I took some of them to a place in Santa Monica where they drew our blood, put it in a glass bottle, and spun ozone into it until it turned bright red, then injected it back into our veins. We practically lived in a far infrared sauna and ate a diet that promoted chelation. People thought we were completely out of our minds, but those of us living it just kept looking and feeling better and younger.

Riviera Recovery was a success. When I had enough saved up, I bought my mom a ticket to Poland so she could visit her family for the first time in over 40 years. When she returned, the trip had jogged her memory enough that she could elaborate on the stories of her childhood—the war, Kazakhstan, Siberia. I had wanted so badly to give her a gift by sending her on that trip, but the gift I received in return was immeasurable. My empathy for her deepened in a way I had never experienced before. So thank you, Mom. And I'm sorry I was such a nightmare...

In a way, my dream of opening up a juice bar had come true on a small scale in the kitchen at Riviera Recovery. I made superfood smoothies every day for most of the clients and it quickly got to the point where there would be 15 people lined up in the morning, waiting for their smoothie. Some of them weren't even clients, just neighbors or kids I sponsored who had tried it once and kept coming back.

Not all of my clients were into all of this. In fact, many were downright obstinate. They got stuck in my place by their parents or by the court and they had no interest in getting better. Those were painful cases and my codependency and insecurity often made me feel like a failure. One girl named Sarah was just about the gnarliest drug addict I'd ever met. In fact, she made my story seem tame in comparison.

When Sarah arrived at Riviera Recovery, she was chain-smoking and loaded up on all kinds of psych meds. She looked like someone needed to take a shovel and bury her. She repeated the same thing all day long: "I don't fucking care, I want to get high. I don't fucking care, I want to get high."

It was her mantra. When she wasn't reciting it, she would stand in the kitchen making fun of us.

"You Malibu people are so fucking stupid with your wheatgrass and your fucking vitamin shots. Everyone here drives a Bentley. This is so stupid. You're all fake. Fuck you."

I loved her anyway. I knew underneath that defiant, harsh façade, she was dying on the inside and missed her kids, who had been taken away from her. She had a huge court case hanging over her head to determine whether or not she would go to jail or get custody of her kids again, and I could see it was ripping her apart. She wanted help. She could have left at any time, but she didn't. So I was going to help her.

It took about six months. Six months of her staying up all night and sleeping through the mornings, smoking constantly, and eating garbage food and candy. But she saw what the rest of us were doing, the effect it had, and one day she came into the kitchen and saw me downing a glass full of liquid vitamins from Premier Research Laboratories that cost about $600 for a month's supply.

"What is that shit?" she said.

"This shit is the best fucking stuff in the world."

"It looks gross," she said.

"Well, I don't drink it because it looks good or tastes good. I drink it because it makes me feel fucking amazing."

That was something she could finally relate to. Meth and

heroin don't taste good, either, but she took them because they made her feel good.

"Can I have a glass?" she asked.

I was surprised, but I immediately grabbed an empty glass and poured a double dose of all the different bottles into it. Sarah downed it and walked away. Two minutes later she was back.

"Can I have another glass?"

"No," I said, "you can't have another fucking glass."

"Why? That really did make me feel better."

"Yeah, that's what I've been trying to tell you for months."

"No, I'm serious," she said. "I really feel good."

"That's just the start. That ain't shit compared to how you'd feel if you really started eating healthy."

"What else is there?"

"I'll make you a smoothie."

I made her a smoothie with raw colostrum, raw almond butter, dates, raw honey, bee pollen, and Royal Jelly in it. She sucked it down without saying a word, but I could tell by the look on her face how it made her feel and how much her body resonated with it.

The next morning she knocked on my door, waking me up. "Can you please make me one of those shakes?"

Within a few weeks, she quit smoking. After two months, against doctor's orders, she stopped all psych meds. The transformation in her could only be described as miraculous. I absolutely fell in love with her—Hayley and I both did and both of us developed an incredible bond and friendship with her. Today she lives in a beautiful home with all of her kids.

It's been almost seven years since she's had a drink or done a drug. She's one of my best friends to this day, a great mom, and after many years of putting her parents through hell, she's now a great daughter. Her parents love her dearly, especially her father, Steven, who is also a great friend and mentor of mine. The four of us go on a trip every January to celebrate the miracle of her recovery. She goes to church twice a week and last year, she started the first organic farmer's market in the town where she lives.

It doesn't get any better than that.

✳ ✳ ✳

As much as I loved helping people, it began to take a toll on me. There was no limit to what I would do for someone who wanted to get sober and healthy and stay that way. Participating in their recovery was a magical experience. But some people simply had no interest in changing. They wanted their toys back, their boyfriends/girlfriends/spouses/houses, or they wanted to get the courts off their back or get their parents to stop harassing them, so they checked into sober living, but they had no interest in truly changing. A lot of these people did what we call "The Tour" in Malibu. They would check into a place like Promises for a quick 30 day spin-dry, although many of them wouldn't even last that long. Then their family would put them right back into another $60,000-a-month treatment center and repeat the process all over again. It wasn't uncommon to have clients who had been to 10 or 15 rehab centers over the course of 5 years.

If people really want to change, they can, but what it comes down to is surrendering. Anybody can be compliant for a certain period of time. In fact, drug addicts and alcoholics are masters at wearing masks and people-pleasing. But to be in a state of surrender takes humility, not a common trait for people of my kind. We get into trouble, swear to God we'll never do it again, pray for help, and make what seem like iron-clad resolutions to our innermost selves and the rest of the world. And then the ego kicks in with its incredible ability to bypass experience and we are, yet again, drunk and high. Because deep down we never really wanted to change in the first place.

I saw it all the time at Riviera Recovery. People would come in with their tails between their legs and make me 10,000 promises about how all they wanted was to be clean and sober and live a good life and would I please help them. Then as soon as their bags were unpacked and their parents were back on a plane to wherever they'd come from, they would start breaking the rules, missing curfew, refusing to go to meetings, etc.

Some were downright toxic people—spiritual vampires living in a constant state of misery and too lazy to do anything about it, so they would just inflict pain upon others and cause constant drama. It started to sicken my soul. Families paid me to help these clients get clean and I knew they were going to put forth zero effort, make no progress, and eventually get high. It ate away at me. It felt like blood money. They sucked the life and enthusiasm out of the clients who really did want to change, then they'd go off, relapse, and go back to another rehab or sober living and start all over.

After five years, Riviera Recovery started to become a dark place for me. I started noticing more and more grey hairs and had constant pain in my neck and lower back, not to mention the stress it put on my relationship with Hayley, who was fed up to the point of no return.

The final straw for me was when one of my best friends who was running the place for me stopped caring. He simply stopped following through and let things fall apart. I wouldn't have cared if it were just an employee but, like I said, he was one of my best friends. I loved him and couldn't understand why he was acting the way he was. I later found out that he had relapsed and had been getting high the whole time.

I sold Riviera Recovery for pennies on the dollar to a guy who grew up very poor in Malibu. He and I had gotten high together years before, and he, like I had, had gotten sober and was doing great. He had heard that I was trying to sell and asked me if he and his partner could buy it from me. They didn't have a lot of money, but I didn't care. I thought it was great that a guy who had a similar background as I did and had come from very humble beginnings was going to take it over. He and his business partner have done an amazing job with the place ever since. I go to 12-step meetings there and run into him quite often.

There were many times in my life when I'd gone through a major change without any idea of what I was going to do next. Dropping out of high school. Moving from Ohio to California. Getting fired from The Canyon.

Not this time.

This time, I knew exactly what I was going to do.

✳   ✳   ✳

By 2011, a bunch of vacant spots had opened up in an old strip mall in Malibu called the Point Dume Village. The mall's new owner had evicted a dive bar and a few other tenants, and the entire complex was in dire need of something fresh.

It was time to make my dream come true. It was time to open SunLife Organics. SunLife— life in the sun. And for its symbol, I would use the pink lotus, a beautiful flower that rises up from the filth and mud.

As with every other thing in my life I've had passion for— music, women, drugs—I became relentless in my pursuit of opening an organic, all-natural juice bar. I was obsessed with making it happen, despite the fact that I had no business plan, no financing, and no idea how to operate a food service business. It never would have happened without Hayley's help, but in the interest of full disclosure, along the way it almost tore us apart.

A few months in, the stress of opening the business caused the biggest fight we've ever had. I was scared of failing and needed someone to blame, so I yelled at her and told her to take the money that was in the safe and get out of my house and out of my life. It was yet another instance of me trying to end things on my terms before it happened anyway, out of my control. Old habits die hard.

Hayley slept in the spare room that night and in the morning she told me, "Don't ever talk to me like that again."

"Okay," I said. It never happened again.

Thank God she stuck with me.

The economy was still caving in at the time and it seemed like it would never recover, but we didn't let that faze us. We just kept pushing forward with our plan of sourcing the most amazing ingredients and produce on the planet, hiring local kids and paying them well, and having a place where friends and neighbors could come together as a community.

I kept telling Hayley, "If we can get 100 customers a day, we'll make it."

Why 100? I have no idea. I never ran projections or profit/loss metrics, nor did I know what either of those were. I just figured that 100 people sounded like a lot, but it didn't sound too lofty.

One year and many speed bumps later, we were ready to open the doors.

"One hundred people." I kept repeating, mostly for myself. "Just 100. That's all we need."

The day before we opened, a school bus parked outside and unloaded dozens of kids. They rushed toward the door and tried to come inside but it was locked. I was about to tell them we weren't open yet, but their faces were so excited and happy, I couldn't turn them away.

Their chaperone hurried over and tried to herd the kids away. "Come on, You guys. Leave them alone. They aren't even open yet."

"No, no. It's fine," I said. "I'll make them stuff."

"No, don't be silly," she said. "You don't need to do that."

"I know, I want to."

"Okay," she said. "I have money for whatever they buy."

"Don't worry about it. The register doesn't even work yet. Come on in."

I think I was more excited than the kids. Someone actually wanted to come into our store! We blended up a bunch of smoothies and we served them with organic frozen yogurt. The kids were so sweet and polite, and the woman kept thanking us.

"We're just happy you guys are here," I said.

After we'd served everybody the kids walked outside. Hayley and I and the couple of kids we had working with us finally had a chance to catch our breath, and we couldn't stop smiling. It was sort of surreal to finally see the dream in action.

The chaperone came back inside. "It's a beautiful day out. Can you come outside for a second? The kids want to say thank you."

We walked outside and the kids were all gathered together. Without warning they broke into beautiful *a capella* singing. They were a Gospel choir and they sang their appreciation in glorious harmony. People from the other businesses came out to listen. Tears ran down my face. We were opening our doors the next day and I had been stressing out over the idea that we might not have a single customer.

As those children sang, I thought, *This is going to work. I really think this is going to work.*

I couldn't sleep that night. We got to SunLife Organics the next morning at 5:00 a.m., three hours before we were scheduled to open. I didn't want to be disappointed, so I'd tempered my goal of 100 people.

*Please just let 20 people show up. Please just let **someone** show up.*

At 7:00 am, a man walked up to the door and looked in.

I ran over and unlocked the door. "Hey, you're our first customer!"

"Customer?" he said "I'm not your customer. I don't even know what this is."

"This is SunLife Organics."

"Well, what does that mean?"

"Uh," I said, "it means life in the sun, and—"

"No, what do you sell? I don't even know what you have here. I was on my way to Subway for breakfast and I just wanted to look in."

"*Subway?*" I said. "No. I'll make you something."

I made him a Green Man, one of our signature recipes, a smoothie full of strawberries, bananas, kale, apple juice, and greens powder. He watched me make it with a look of skepticism.

"I've never had a smoothie before," he said.

"Good thing you're starting out with the best."

"But I don't like vegetables."

"You'll like this."

He took a tiny sip, then a big gulp. "This is great!"

"Why do you seem so surprised?" I asked.

"Because it looked disgusting. But you were right, it's delicious, and I am officially your first customer."

I didn't want to take his money, but he insisted. It turned out he was a dentist with a practice nearby, and he's come in every single day since then. He was our first customer and remains one of our biggest fans. You can see many of the articles that he's written about us on MalibuPatch.com.

With the day off to such a good start, I let myself dream a little bit: maybe we would hit 100 customers. When we officially opened the doors at 8:00 a.m., there was a line waiting outside. We served over 250 people that day.

We still had plenty of rough spots that needed smoothing, but our customers were incredibly patient and supportive. Thank God for them, and for the beautiful kids who work there who have made SunLife Organics what it is. They embody everything I'd hoped it could be and more. Because of their brilliant energy and passion for life, the dream has evolved into something far greater than I ever could have imagined.

Today there are four SunLife Organics, with a fifth in

the works, and all of them are thriving. A recent seven-figure deal ensures that six more stores will be open by 2017. I employ over 130 people today, which is a miracle in itself considering where I was 12 years ago and that I myself am literally unemployable.

Yoga is still a huge part of my life. As a matter of fact, I opened up my own yoga studio a couple of years ago right above the original SunLife Organics, called Malibu Beach Yoga. It was another way I could be of service to the community but it also ensures that I stay practicing. One of the main instructors there is Jennifer's sister.

* * *

There is only the straight and narrow. It's sort of silly that it took me so long to come to this conclusion. I searched for years—decades in fact. I experimented with massive amounts of hallucinogens and other drugs. I did all the different forms of yoga and breath work. I bought all the books, dabbled in all the religions, saw healers and shamans, travelled to vortexes, bought tens of thousands of dollars' worth of crystals and devices I thought would heal me: lasers, singing bowls, pendants and bracelets, CDs and MP3s on meditation. I traveled all over India for weeks on end. I spent a month in Indonesia going from island to island doing yoga and chanting. I've been hugged by so-called living Saints and took the Transcendental Meditation course.

In the end, there is only the straight and narrow. The only thing I ever needed to know was written in the Bible and that is to love God before all else and to love my neighbor as I love myself. That's it; that's the whole truth. There's nothing more I ever need to know about spirituality or God.

There is only one judge of who I am and what I am and that is my Creator. I believe all of us will be quite shocked when we take our final breath and find our convictions shattered to pieces by the real, unifying truth of our timeless existence. But for now, here on this earth, I am glad to finally understand that there is only the straight and narrow—the path of love, truth, compassion, kindness, and hard work. Each day I fall short of the mark, but each morning when I am blessed with another try I make a pact with myself to do my best.

It makes me really sad to think how close I came to missing it all. I turned my life into such a mess that I couldn't even kill myself correctly. And in the midst of all of that madness, all of that grace, and all of the beautiful recovery that has taken place in the last 12 years, I forgot to die.

Now I will always remember to live.

ABOUT THE AUTHOR

KHALIL RAFATI is a speaker, author, and health-and-wellness entrepreneur. He has been a dog walker, a nanny, a car detailer, a furniture maker, a rehab counselor, a restaurant manager, and a drug dealer. Today, he is the owner of Malibu Beach Yoga and SunLife Organics, a rapidly growing chain of popular juice and smoothie bars in California. He also founded Riviera Recovery, a transitional living facility for drug addicts and alcoholics, and is a board member of the Tashi Lhunpo Monastery in Bylakuppe, India.